T0094844

THE
PERFORMANCE
HANDBOOK
FOR
MUSICIANS,
SINGERS
AND ALL
PERFORMERS

THE PERFORMANCE HANDBOOK FOR MUSICIANS, SINGERS AND ALL PERFORMERS

CLAUDE WEBSTER

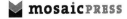 **mosaic**PRESS

Library and Archives Canada Cataloguing in Publication

Title: The performance handbook: for musicians, singers, and all performers / by Claude Webster; foreword by Yannick Nezet-Seguin.
Names: Webster, Claude, author. | Nézet-Séguin, Yannick, 1975- writer of foreword.

Identifiers: Canadiana (print) 20200293966 | Canadiana (ebook) 20200294059 | ISBN 9781771615006 (softcover) | ISBN 9781771615013 (PDF) | ISBN 9781771615020 (EPUB) | ISBN 9781771615037 (Kindle) | Subjects: LCSH: Music—Performance—Psychological aspects. | LCSH: Singing—Psychological aspects. | LCSH: Performance anxiety.

Classification: LCC ML3830 .W378 2020 | DDC 781.4/3111—dc2

All rights reserved. Without limiting the rights under copyright reserved here, no part of this publication may be reproduced, stored in or introduced into any retrieval system, or transmitted in any form or by any means—electronic, mechanical, by photocopy, recording or otherwise—without the prior written permission and consent of both the copyright owners and the Publisher of this book.

Published by Mosaic Press, Oakville, Ontario, Canada, 2021.

MOSAIC PRESS, Publishers
Copyright © Claude Webster, 2021
Printed and bound in Canada.

Designed by Andrea Tempesta • www.flickr.com/photos/andreatempesta

ONTARIO ARTS COUNCIL
CONSEIL DES ARTS DE L'ONTARIO
an Ontario government agency
un organisme du gouvernement de l'Ontario

Funded by the Government of Canada
Financé par le gouvernement du Canada

Canadä

We acknowledge the Ontario Arts Council
for their support of our publishing program

MOSAIC PRESS
1252 Speers Road, Units 1 & 2, Oakville, Ontario, L6L 5N9
(905) 825-2130 • info@mosaic-press.com • www.mosaic-press.com

The information and suggestions contained in this book are not intended to replace medical advice and should be used to supplement rather than replace the services of your healthcare professionals. Because each person and each medical situation is unique, your individual's health concerns should be evaluated by a qualified professional. The publisher and the author disclaim liability for any medical outcomes that may occur as a result of applying the methods suggested in this book.

This handbook is dedicated to you,
may you find here the inspiration you need
to express yourself freely.

PREFACE

by Yannick Nézet-Séguin

I met Claude Webster in 1998 when he was a pianist for the Montreal Opera. I was twenty-three, and had just arrived as chorus master. We worked together with great pleasure for several years, over the course of which we collaborated with many artists, singers in particular, who were often nervous and unsatisfied with their performances. Both of us were preoccupied with helping them improve.

I am therefore overjoyed that Claude shifted his career towards a systematic understanding of this unique set of challenges, and I very eagerly accepted to write a preface to the summary of his conclusions.

In his book, Claude speaks to all those who feel stress and anxiety when faced with giving a performance. With the help of examples and suitable exercises, he guides such a person in his or her battle with their fears to reach a point of "knowing inner calm". Claude offers a means to enter into oneself and to take advantage — physically, mentally, and emotionally — of all the conscious and unconscious resources of one's brain in order to replace nervousness and anxiety with pleasure.

In the world of music, this book is truly invaluable, as the pressure to offer the perfect performance is all too common. Often obsessed by the fear of a mediocre performance, musicians and singers sometimes forget the primary goals of music: the creation of beauty, communicating something to an audience for the purpose of moving them, and deriving pleasure and satisfaction from this exchange. Stress can wreak havoc, not only through its negative influence on the performance of music, but above all psychologically on the performer him or herself, destroying an artist who, after years of sustained pressure and misery, may choose to abandon music altogether.

Music being a metaphor for life, the same stress can manifest itself in other domains and other spheres. Work of whatever kind brings its share of frustrations and anxieties. Who hasn't experienced the fear of performing poorly in an interview, in an evaluation, or as spokesperson for a committee? And who hasn't experienced symptoms of stress such as clammy hands, weak legs or butterflies in the stomach before a life-changing encounter?

This book is meant not only for artists, but also for businesspeople, teachers, public speakers — in short, to everyone who must give a performance, no matter what kind.

Having been forced to learn, at the beginning of my career, how to manage terrible stress on my own, I would have really benefited from a guide like this one!

Yannick Nézet-Séguin
Music Director, The Metropolitan Opera (New York)
Music Director, The Philadelphia Orchestra
Artistic Director and Principal Conductor, Orchestre Métropolitain de Montréal

INTRODUCTION

As musicians, we spend countless weeks, months and years practicing our instruments. It is a relief and an accomplishment to be able to perform our selected repertoire exactly the way we want. But what we are ultimately after, is to be able to deliver it on Thursday afternoon at 3:30, because that is our audition slot, our exam or the first round of a competition. Suddenly the stakes are higher and a different kind of pressure grows.

It is almost taboo for musicians to talk about stress. We often prefer to make jokes or act as if everything is fine; to talk earnestly about our difficulties with stress, anxiety or staying concentrated would mean that there is something wrong with us.

When you are working on a new piece and run into a technical difficulty, you go to your teacher to figure out how to work through it. If you have to sing a piece in Russian or German, you get the help of a linguist, or a specialist in those languages. If your new piece is of a musical style you have never done before, you take it to a musical coach.

Nobody hesitates or is ashamed to ask for such varieties of help. It is a normal part of the process of becoming an accomplish musician. Yet a performer will also face auditions, premières, debuts, important concerts, maybe even competitions, and stress will be an integral part of the life too. Why are we afraid to ask for help in facing these very real challenges too? Understanding and learning how to deal with the pressure and the stress of performance is as vital a skill to master as technique, style and diction.

Some people use to believe that "you either have it or you don't". Fortunately, that type of mentality is gradually changing. It is just like playing your instrument: it can be learned, improved and mastered.

I am very excited to share with you all the tools I have discovered and tested with thousands of musicians and singers I have worked with over the years in this profession. My goal with this book is to help you give your best when under pressure—and ultimately, to raise your level of pleasure and enjoyment during all of your performances.

But first, let me introduce myself and tell you how I got where I am today.

From Pianist to...

I am a pianist.

I have always loved playing the piano. Even as a child, from the very first time my fingers rendered the notes written on the score into sound, I was fascinated. I had the impression that I was performing a magic ritual and entering into a sacred world. Still, it took years before I became a pianist.

During my university studies, I participated in numerous piano competitions. Competitions are a normal part of the journey of a young aspiring pianist, a rite of passage that one goes through in order to be recognized, to make a name for oneself and to built a career.

One of these national competitions was allegedly "rigged." I was told that you had to know a member of the jury in order to win. Not knowing anyone in the panel, I thought: "I don't stand a chance, but since I know all the required repertoire, it will be a good practice for future competitions." I entered and played stress-free during the first round.

To my surprise, I was admitted to the semi-finals. I said to myself, "What a surprise to have gotten through! I think I played well, but I still don't have a chance." I played at the semi-final for the sheer pleasure of playing, without an afterthought. I noticed that the jury members were talking amongst themselves a great deal during my recital. I was sure they were commenting on everything they did not like. I was unknown to them, and so I thought they did not appreciate my way of playing. Instead of disturbing me, however, this thought completely liberated me. I had a friend in the audience, and I played for her.

The next day, I was surprised to learn that I was one of the finalists. One of the organizers came to congratulate me, saying that hands down, I would win the competition. Catastrophe! Inside me, an incredible stress arose. The expectations of the jury weighed down on my shoulders like a ton of bricks. At the finals, I played Tchaikovsky's first piano concerto, at war with myself. I was stuck in a dark cloud and had no way out. I did not play badly, but I was far from the comfort, confidence, and pleasure that I had felt during the first two rounds. The result: the jury didn't give a first prize, and I was awarded second place.

If you think that this was an enriching challenge, that I learned some important lessons and was then able to give the best of myself and win other competitions, you are going to be disappointed since that is only half true. At that time, there was not much help for these kinds of difficulties. Either you were good on stage or you went into teaching.

And yet I felt deep within me that with experience, time, and a little help, I could improve. Determined to make a name for myself as a pianist, I rolled up my sleeves and dove into other competitions, all the while reading as many books as possible, doing yoga, meditating, taking care of my body, my diet, and so on.

It did help: I managed to win a good number of prizes in various competitions. I placed second or third at many. But during all those years, managing the pressure remained a challenge.

It is thanks to these competitions that I discovered and gradually began using different strategies to stay in control during my performances. This allowed me to start a nice career with several recital tours, playing with renowned orchestras, and even make an important dream of mine come true: doing my New York *début* recital, with an excellent review in the New York Times.

In my early thirties, my life as a young concert pianist was very exciting and glamorous but lacked any financial stability. There were no teaching positions available but there was an opening at the *Opera de Montréal* so I took the apprentice pianist/coach position as a try out for a year—and it changed my life. I had accompanied singers throughout my university years and had always loved it, but working at the *Opera de Montréal*, I discovered a world that in the end satisfied me far more than having a career as a soloist. I eventually became the Head Coach of the *Atelier lyrique*—the young artists' program of the *Opéra de Montréal* and later on, became Chorus Master as well. I retired recently after 20 years from the Head Coach position, but still remain Chorus Master.

...Performance Coach

In the mid 2000s, I heard about sports psychologists using NLP to help high-level athletes improve performance. I had no idea what Neuro-Linguistic Programming (NLP) was, but I hoped to find a few, simple tricks that could help manage stress. I was immediately intrigued. I did not think that I would discover such a rich and powerful psychological approach, one with practical tools that went far beyond the scope of handling pressure.

Conceived in the 1970s by two Americans, Richard Bandler and John Grinder, NLP was born of the desire to model excellence. That is, to study people who were expert and succeed brilliantly in one domain. That direction went against the usual tendency of psychology to study pathologies and concentrate on the causes and reasons behind those problems. This revolutionary approach, inspired by the modeling of those experts, proposed simple and concrete tools that work just as well for communication as they do for facilitating change. Those tools completely transformed my approach to coaching singers.

Around the same time I discovered NLP, I started receiving invitations to several international summer programs as a French repertoire vocal specialist. That is when I realized that all the hours I spent coaching singers privately were often lost when they arrived on stage because all of their energy was focused not on the music, but merely on surviving the stress of the performance. They were drowning in stress and too busy keeping their heads above the water to apply what we had worked on together the preceding days. That was when I began giving group classes in order to help them improve the way they dealt with that stress.

Besides my concert activities, work as a vocal coach and Chorus Master at Opéra de Montréal, I became so passionate about developing tools to help young musicians and singers that I became a certified coach/instructor in NLP and Eriksonian hypnosis—and eventually also did a university certificate in psychology.

Little by little I realized that in combining my experience on-stage (all the things I learned on the fly) with the knowledge I gained from NLP, hypnosis, and my university studies in psychology, I could really help people improve their performance.

I began giving workshops on stress management, followed by conferences and training on mental preparation for performance. I experimented, tested, and tried several avenues, and finally, after several years, I believe I have developed an efficient and accessible method that can remarkably improve performance. It was after one of those workshops that I felt the need to put the results of my research in writing.

This book is specifically written for musicians: instrumentalists and singers. It is the revised, improved and upgraded version (with lots of new material) of the one I wrote in French called *Atteindre sa zone d'excellence* (Reaching your Inner Zone of Excellence) in 2016. It is not meant to be the definitive bible of performance preparation, but rather a starting point.

It is dedicated to all of those who, like myself have at one time or another been under the impression that they could not perform to the level of their true potential. Regardless of the form that stress takes, regardless of how long you have been trying to face your fears, there is hope.

"I'll Never Get Stage Fright Again?"

I would love to tell you that I have discovered the secret to never being nervous before or during a performance—but unfortunately, I do not have any miracle cures. I do, however, have a toolbox full of simple and accessible ways for you to reach the level of performance you dream to attain.

My experience as a teacher and coach has shown me that real improvements manifest themselves much more quickly and easily than people think. Often, one thing, one idea, one bit of inspiration is enough to transform your usual reactions when under pressure. There is no magic pill, but the results are even more impressive since they come from within you. You will become the hero of your own journey, and the satisfaction gained from this accomplishment will have consequences on all aspects of your life.

These past few years spent helping others overcome their fears and take back the reins of their performances have allowed me to try out on myself all these tools and to reach a level of pleasure and fulfillment on stage that I previously did not think was even possible.

This does not mean that I am never nervous and that my self-confidence is unshakeable. From time to time, an old demon comes back or a new one appears, as if to remind me that even if I know what to do, when faced with a difficult challenge we still have to face our true selves and there is always room for growth. The difference is that now, I am able to stay in my zone of excellence and deliver a satisfactory performance. Surpassing ourself can only happen by embracing these challenges.

I will invite you to get to know your fears, to understand the messages they send, to clarify and articulate your goals, to learn how to calm your mind, and to create new mental "programs" that will allow you to perform at your best.

There are many ways to use this book. You can just read through it and get an overview at first. The examples will act as a catalyst to open your mind to new possibilities and create changes in your life. In the stories, the names of the instrumentalists or singers were changed to preserve their privacy and some details were modified to prevent any direct identification—as some of them went on to become international stars.

To get the greatest results, you can do the exercises starting with the ones that speak to you the most. Also, listen to your instinct and pace yourself. If one day you feel that you are not in the right mental space to do a particular exercise, come back to it later. You can be committed, perseverant, persistent but there is no need to push yourself through an exercise if it does not feel right at that moment. If you feel that it touches something deep and dark in you, do not hesitate to find someone to help you and guide you through it.

This book is not only a manual to prepare you to face challenges, it is a call to action that will allow you to become the captain of your own ship.

There is hope!

Psychologist Martin Seligman (who later became the founder of the positive psychology movement) did an experiment in 1967 that became a turning point in the history of psychology and the way we conceptualize stress.

In the first part of his study, three groups of dogs were placed in harnesses. The first group was given electric shocks at random times, but the dogs could stop those shocks by pressing a lever. The second group was paired with the first group; whenever a dog of the first group received a shock, its paired dog in the second group got that shock too. But for the second group dogs, those shocks seamed to end at random because they had no way of stopping them. And the third group, the control group, were in harnesses but no shocks were delivered to them. After a while, the second group of dogs started to show symptoms associated with depression, like loss of enthusiasm, energy and appetite, but not the other two groups.

In the second part of the experiment, the same three groups of dogs were tested in a new situation. They were placed, one at a time, in a box with an electric floor. When the shocks were sent again randomly, the dogs looking for an exit realized that behind a low barrier there was another chamber, without an electric floor. By jumping over the low barrier to the other side of the box, the dogs could easily escape those shocks.

Something unexpected happened. The dogs of the first and third groups avoided the shocks immediately by jumping to the other side, the normal response of an animal with the possibility to escape. But the dogs of the second group did not even attempt to avoid them because they had learned that there was nothing they could do, so they endure them passively. Their previous exposure prevented them to access their "normal", adapted strategies when faced with a hostile and uncomfortable situation.

That reaction was called: learned helplessness.

Does it mean that those dogs who had developed that helplessness were condemned to endure it indefinitely? The conclusion of the experiment showed that when the experimenters physically helped the dogs replicate the actions necessary to escape the electric grid at least two times, the dogs would start willfully leaping over the barrier by themselves.

That means that no matter how many bad experiences you have had with your past performances, and how helpless you think you are in managing your nerves, it is just a learned automatism that can be transformed. You need new strategies and a little bit of help to figure out your way across the barrier.

CHAPTER 1
IT'S A MIND GAME

Basic principle of performance preparation -
Entering the flow and paradox of the classical musician

The mystique of rock climbing is climbing; you get to the top of a rock glad it's over but really wishing it would go on forever...You don't conquer anything except things in yourself.... The purpose of the flow is to keep on flowing, not looking for a peak or utopia but staying in the flow. It is not a moving up but a continuous flowing; you move up to keep the flow going. There is no possible reason for climbing except the climbing itself; it is a self-communication.

Mihaly Csikszentmihalyi,

Basic principle:

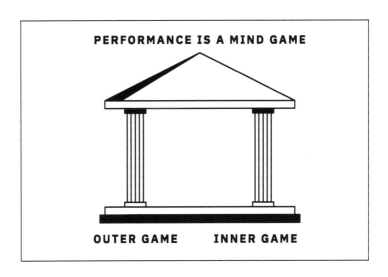

I love to simplify complex processes in order to understand them more easily and make them more user-friendly. That is why I use a simple model to explore the basic dynamic of a performance. We often hear that a performance is a mind game. I agree and I add that within a mind game, there are two pillars.

Imagine a beautiful Greek temple that represent this mind game. The temple is supported by two pillars. One pillar is the outer game. It represents the ability: all the elements involved in the skill necessary to perform (in your case, singing or playing your musical instrument). The other pillar is the inner game. It relates to the psychological aspects of a performance, to what goes on in your head other than the task at hand. Let me give you an example:

If I ask you to pour some tea from a teapot into a cup, the ability (the outer game) is minimal and you are all capable of doing it very easily. If I put the teapot on a small table, on a stage, in a stadium, in front of 50 000 people, with a camera focus on that table, showing you on a huge screen while you still simply have to pour some tea into a cup… the ability is still minimal and simple but suddenly there are some interferences. Suddenly, you have doubts, you are afraid, you start questioning yourself: Will I spill some? What if I start shaking? What will people say? etc. That is the psychological aspect I was talking about—the inner game of that mind game.

In order to counteract the effects of the psychological aspect of poring the tee in front of thousands of people, you could work on your outer game. For example, you could clarify how do you grab the teapot handle exactly:

- Do you hold the cover as you pour?
- Do you breathe in before/during you take the handle?
- Do you hold your breath or do you exhale as you pour?
- How do you stand as you pour the tea?
- How high or low are your shoulders?
- Where do you look just before? During? Etc.

Just by bringing more awareness into your outer game, it will help you focus and stay in the present. That could be all you need to take the stress response down enough to perform at your best. The same idea will apply for a musical performance.

For musicians and singers, the ability—or if you prefer the skill- necessary to play your instrument is extremely complex. It involves a multitude of reflexes and takes many years to learn, integrate, and master. I could also add that it is an ability that will never be finished in the sense that you can improve it all your life. A never-ending process. I'll explore with you these outer game aspects of the preparation in the Goals of Action section.

One of the key elements of performance preparation is to make the link between the actions required for your ability and the psychological aspects. I will propose a map in Chapter 3 called the Pyramid of a Musician, which will help you clarify these actions and those automatisms. Once they are more conscious, they can act as a doorway to help you enter the flow or as I like to call it, your inner zone of excellence.

What is this flow state?

When you perform at your best, you probably have experienced a state of bliss, of immense satisfaction where all seems to happen harmoniously. You may have heard it called a peak experience, being in the flow, being in the zone or even the runner's high. Hungarian psychologist Mihaly Csikszentmihalyi (pronounced me-high, chick-send-me-high), was the first to use the term *flow*. In his book: *Flow: The Psychology of Optimal Experience,* he describes the fruit of his twenty-five years of research on optimal experience and its application in daily life.

During his interviews, many subjects kept using the term *flow* to describe this optimal state of performance in which the activity was effortless, fluid, flowy. He defined that state as *"being completely involved in an activity for its own sake. The ego falls away. Time flies. Every action, movement and thought follows inevitably from the previous one, like playing jazz. Your whole being is involved, and you are using your skills to the utmost."*

The most recent research by Steven Kotler at the Flow Genome Project has made many interesting discoveries in their studies of flow. They consider flow as *"an optimal state of consciousness, a peak state where we both feel our best and perform our at best."* [1]

That flow state can best be described as effortless, selfless and timeless.

Effortless:

I often hear musicians or singers mention that when they are performing at their best, they do nothing and it is so easy. I understand what they mean but in reality, they are not "doing nothing". The actions are so clear, the automatization of those actions is so fluid that they have the impression of doing nothing. In reality, their actions have a clear goal

---

1 Steven Kotler, *The Rise of Superman*, P.viii

and the immediate feedback allows them to readjust constantly and easily during the activity. There is an absence of struggle but not an absence of actions.

I like to compare this process to driving a car. At the beginning, you can be overwhelmed by all the action needed, but gradually you integrate them and after a while, they become so automatic that you may even have the impression that you are "doing nothing." But if you were doing nothing, the car would not move! It's the same idea when you play a musical instrument. It requires a perfectly planned and partially automatic physical effort.

That perfectly planned goal will have a great impact on your intensity of focus. Daniel Simons from the University of Illinois did an experiment on the mechanism of attention that clearly demonstrated how a clear goal impacts attention.

He showed a group of students a short video of a basketball game in which the students were asked to count the number of passes. After the film, Simons asked, how many of you saw the gorilla? In the middle of the clip, a guy dressed in a gorilla costume walked on the court and beat his chest a couple of times before walking off. Most of the students did not see the gorilla at all because *"When the brain is charged with a clear goal, focus narrows considerably, the unimportant is disregarded, and the now is all that is left."* [2]

Another interesting element is that the actions required are neither too easy (you would get bored) nor too difficult (you would get discouraged).

To assimilate that knowledge, I'll explore how to clarify those goals of action during a musical performance in Chapter 3.

Selfless:

When you are totally absorbed in the activity, all distractions disappear and there is no place left for any inner dialogue not linked to the activity. This total involvement weakens the frontier of your inner self to the point of becoming one with the activity. That feeling frees you from the need to compare yourself with others, since all that matters is to stay focused on the task at hand.

During flow, the part of the brain responsible for self-monitoring goes quiet. That inner negative and nagging voice in your head; that never satisfied inner perfectionist, is shut off because flow is an action state. You are free from the need to compare yourself with others. Any second-guessing would just slow you down. You can act freely, and your creativity can take over.

2   Steven Kotler, *The Rise of Superman*, P.114

Chapter 4 will explore more in depth this notion of focusing your thoughts.

Timeless:

When you are in the Flow, when your sense of self starts to fade away, your perception of time is also affected. The technical term is time dilatation. *In general, most people report that time seems to pass much faster. But occasionally the reverse occurs.*[3] You may even feel as if you are outside a temporal frame, as if time stopped.

The same part of the brain responsible for the selfless effect also distort your experience of time. The energy your brain would need to process time is redirected for attention and awareness. One of the positive impacts of this process is that since there are no past and no future, you are free of expectations and results. All that counts is to stay in the present moment—in the now.

Since being in the Flow is an action state, his biggest enemy is fear. Your fears will prevent you to access this effortless, selfless and timeless state. The importance of disarming, redirecting or transforming your fears will be explored in Chapter 5: Facing your fears.

FLOW STATE
INNER ZONE OF EXCELLENCE

EFFORTLESS
clear goals &
Feedback and adjustments

•

TIMELESS
time dilatation,
free from past/future,
in the now

•

SELFLESS
100% absorb,
feel one with the activity
Focus/Concentration

---

3   Mihaly Csikszentmihalyi, *Flow: The Psychology of Optimal Experience*

> **When beating the opponent takes precedence in the mind over performing as well as possible, enjoyment tends to disappear. Competition is enjoyable only when it is a means to perfect one's skills; when it becomes an end in itself, it ceases to be fun.**
>
> *Mihaly Csikszentmihalyi*

One important thing to understand about Flow is that it is not like a light switch: on or off. It is more fluid than that. If, during a performance, you realize that you are watching yourself (and no longer making music), it is normal and it is time to use for example your goals of action (see Chapter 3) to get back into Flow.

Often, young musicians when they perform, stay relatively well in the Flow but as soon as they make a mistake they give up and go on automatic pilot, letting the automatisms take over. They need to plan ahead thinking of what to do if a mistake happens and to understand that they can get back in the Flow as easily as they left it. They can develop the skill that will allow them to make a mistake without letting it highjack their concentration.

Finally, Steven Kotler propose that Flow can be best understand as a four-part cycle:
The first step is known as struggle or chaos,
The second step is release,
The third is the Flow state itself,
The fourth is recovery.

The first step is a loading phase that every musician knows too well. It is the preparation phase where you overload your brain with information. I like the fact that they call it struggle because it makes it normal and okay that it requires lots of work and effort when we practice. That loading is about the clarification and installation of all the automatisms necessary to excel as a classical musician. It can also refer to the stress you feel just before a performance with lots of chemical changes taking place inside of you with stress hormones like adrenaline and cortisol pumping through your system. How you handle that stress will be critical to access the Flow.

But to move out of struggle and enter the flow state there is a doorway to enter. The **second step** is the release or letting go of all the previous struggle. Whether it takes the form of relaxation, a decision or an act of faith, will depend on your own preference. You will find many different ideas in the last-minute tools or in the calming of your inner dialogue chapter. It is an ability that you will be able to develop like any other skill, with a good plan and repetitions.

The third step is the actual Flow itself: that effortless, selfless and timeless state. You lose yourself in the task, and the pleasure of juggling all those actions is exhilarating.

The fourth and final step in the cycle is recovery. The energy required to produce and maintain the flow state is enormous and it takes some time to return to normal. It is a transition from being on top of the world, to feel like superman, and to return to a more down-to-earth reality. *It can take a considerable amount of resilience to navigate recovery.* [4]

> ## «Don't ask what the world needs. Ask what makes you come alive. Because what the world needs most is more people who have come alive».
>
> *Howard Thurman.*

In summary: when you perform you enter a mind game. That mind game is composed of two major elements, your ability (outer game) and the interferences in your head (inner game). Both elements need to be addressed in some specific ways in order for you to enter Flow. That Flow state or your inner zone of excellence is a safe place, a protected space that shields you from interferences.

Interference to Flow

Imagine that a performance is like the weather. Sometimes the sun shines, it is a beautiful day and all is going your way. Maybe you can explain it: you were well prepared, or you are not very nervous about this event, or maybe you cannot explain it really. Other times, it is cloudy, the rain starts, the wind is picking up, and you have to work to stay focused.

The rain and the winds are what I call interferences. In your everyday life, bad weather may slow you down a little, but do you stay home? No, you take an umbrella and

---

4   Steven Kotler, *The Rise of Superman*, P.122

you go out. And if the wind blows very hard and closes your umbrella, you re-open it and keep going where you are headed. In a performance, it is the same.

The interference takes the form of fear, doubt, criticism, judgement, the end result like winning or losing, your expectations, your teacher's expectations and even the ghosts of previous performances. These are like the rain and the wind. I will propose that you build an umbrella to keep yourself dry, in a safe space: your inner zone. And you will also need to develop the necessary strength to keep the umbrella open or to re-open it if the winds are too strong.

To help you build that I will use three different angles: the clarification of your goals, the calming of your mental activity and the transformation of you fears. After many years of workshops with musicians and singers, I realized that it is a better strategy to start our exploration with some very effective and concrete tools to disarm the stress just before you go on stage with my last- minute tools.

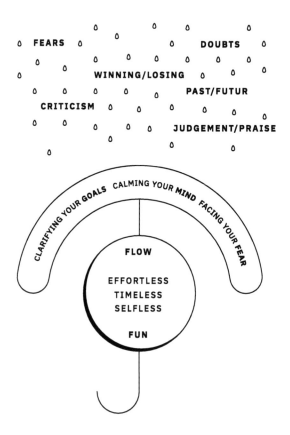

I wrote this book with the chapters in a specific order. But feel free to navigate according to your own needs of the moment. If you prefer to start with calming your inner dialogue or facing your fears, just follow your instinct.

MY PERSONAL EXPERIENCE OF THE FLOW

Performing in front of an audience became a significant part of my life early on. During adolescence, I had the chance to experience moments of going beyond myself in situations that were initially very stressful. Thanks to my instinct, which guided me, I was able to regularly give the best of myself when I was in front of the public. This was probably what gave me the "bug" for the stage.

It was when I was about seventeen and beginning college that I first noticed the pressures, expectations, and fears that could arise in performances. I worked very hard to overcome these interferences. Gradually, one step at a time, I began to master my inner world. I experienced moments of great satisfaction but also of great disappointment and discouragement.

Near the end of my university studies, I had the impression that several important elements were finally starting to fall into place. Through relentless work and many experiences, I acquired a greater mastery of instrumental technique, as well as the confidence necessary to manage stress and give the best of myself in performance.

I decided to enter a prestigious competition (a different one from that mentioned in my Introduction). I was musically, technically, and mentally well prepared, and I felt that I was in full possession of my faculties. I played the first piece, a sonata by Haydn, and everything went well. Then, Chopin's Sonata no.2 op.35 in four movements. The further into the piece I got, the more I felt I was entering an altered state. It was a state wherein everything seemed easy, where things flowed by themselves, where I was under the impression that the music was moving through me in a more intense way than usual.

During the third movement, all of a sudden, I had the impression that my will to do what I had planned gave way to a current of energy that seemed to come directly from the music. I felt like a tightrope walker high up in the air, moving with disconcerting ease. The feeling was absolutely incredible. It is also very difficult to describe. Time seemed to have stopped, and I entered into another dimension: a force much greater than me was moving through my body and taking over. Kind of like a medium who lets a spirit speak through him, but entirely conscious that it was in fact I who was playing. I analyzed nothing, I simply took advantage and abandoned myself to this incredible emotional intensity.

At the end of the performance, the reaction and comments of the spectators confirmed that something special had happened. "This must be what they call a moment of grace," I said to myself.

I did not win first prize but came in second. Surprisingly, the result did not upset me at all. What I had just experienced, and the public's reaction had moved me so much that I felt at peace and was fulfilled.

That magical moment has served as my guidepost—like a lighthouse showing me the way. I had the chance to relive that kind of moment several times in my life. Experience has taught me that I cannot arrive at this state through sheer willpower. The magic happens when I face what has to be done, I believe in myself, and I let the music move through me. It is thanks to this significant performance that I discovered that I play the piano because it allows me to be in touch with something greater than myself.

The Importance of a Regular Practice

We are what we do repeatedly. Excellence, then, is not an act but a habit.

Aristotle

Throughout this book, to help you enter this Flow state on demand, I will present some powerful ideas. Whether it is about calming your inner negative voice, clarifying your goals or transforming your fears, developing new habits might take some time. There is a beautiful saying in Indonesia: Knowledge is only a rumor until it is in the muscles. To understand how things work is not enough. You need to put them into action, one step at a time.

I want to remind you to give yourself a chance and have patience. Just as when you want to get back into physical shape, you do not go to the gym once a week for three hours; you get greater results if you go several times a week for a shorter period of time. You create a regular practice by taking smaller steps. Just like you did to learn to play your instrument.

Here is a story adapted from Steven Chandler's *100 Ways to Motivate Yourself*, to remind you of the importance of those small steps.

DRIBBLING WITH THE LEFT HAND

When I coach basketball, if one of the kids uses the same hand all the time to dribble, he is at a disadvantage when faced with an opponent. And so, I tell him, "to face your opponent, you have to alternate constantly between the left and right hands, that way your opponent has fewer chances of intercepting the ball."

"I can't." the kid usually says.
"What do you mean?" I ask, smiling.
He then shows me that he is not as good with the non-dominant hand.
I then tell him, "It's not that you can't, you just haven't done it enough. You have to form a new habit."

With enough time and practice, the kid will discover that he is able to dribble just as well with either hand.

The same principal is true for reprogramming our own dominant habits of thinking. If our normal inner dialogue is negative and pessimistic, all we have to do is train ourselves to dribble with the other hand; in other words, thinking optimistic thoughts more and more often until it becomes natural.

If someone had asked me years ago why I didn't try to be more optimistic, I would have answered, "because I can't. That's not who I am. I wouldn't know how, I wouldn't feel sincere, authentic."

But it would have been more accurate to answer, "Because I haven't done it enough."

During my years of working with musicians and singers, I always felt the balance between being meticulous and rigorous with all the details and different variables involved in making music versus the freedom and emotional intensity necessary for an outstanding performance, was often two contradictory forces at play. Here is another way of looking at it:

The paradox of the classical musician

How long does it take to become a professional classical musician or singer and what do you need to achieve it? Maybe you have heard the saying: it takes 10 000 hours to become an expert!

In the 1990, psychologist Anders Ericsson conducted research on expertise that has shown that it takes at least ten years in order to attain an international level of performance in most sport and the arts—as well as in other work areas.

Ericsson's research at the Music Academy of Berlin (Hochschule der Kuenste) found that although an early musical environment was helpful what really made the difference between average, good and excellent players was the number of hours spend practicing their instrument. To be more specific, to achieve an international level of expertise, the key factor is the amount of "deliberate practice".

Deliberate practice is described as a period of training in which the explicit aim is to improve performance. These highly structured training sessions require effort, determination and concentration and are not inherently enjoyable.[5]

In contrast to just playing your instrument for the fun of it, deliberate, well-structured practice is a rigorous approach to mastery that needs to be carried out over extended periods of time. This type of practice under the guidance of another expert includes many aspects with emphasis on conscious performance monitoring and identifying "errors"—with strategies to eliminate them.

How do you sustain your motivation for such an extended number of years? Let us take a look at a famous and enlightening experience: the marshmallows experiment.

In 1972, Stanford psychologist, Walter Mischel conducted a study on delayed gratification on four-year-old kids. He offered one marshmallow to a kid with the choice to either eat it right away or to wait while Mischel ran a small errand then receive two marshmallows as a reward.

Some kids waited while many could not resist and ate the marshmallow right away. When they interviewed the same kids years later, the follow-up showed that the kids who waited were more confident, hardworking, could handle stress better and scored higher on their SATs than the kids who did not or could not wait.

The kids who ate the marshmallows immediately were labeled "present hedonists". They lived for the now. We may be tempted to judge them as being weak. But there is a bright side of this personality trait: those individuals are creative, spontaneous, open-minded, high-energy risk-takers who play sports, have hobbies, make friends easily. Their lives are fun-filled and fast-paced. Unfortunately, all that comes at a cost. In the extreme case, they

5 Deakin, J.M., Cote, J., & Harvey, S. A. *The Influence of Experience and Deliberate Practice on the Development of Superior Expert Performance,*

tend to act without anticipating consequences, and they don't learn from past failures. They have a fondness for the wild side of life, with the pitfalls that usually comes with it.

The kids who did not eat the marshmallow were called "future-oriented". They are able to resist temptation today for a chance at a greater reward tomorrow. They outperform "present hedonists" in dozens of studies. They consider work a source of special pleasure while the present hedonists tend to avoid work altogether. We could make a generalization and say that the "presents" live in their bodies while the "futures" live more in their heads.

The paradox

Futures are more likely to achieve the 10,000 hours needed for mastery, with all the deliberate and very structured practices. In the process they will most likely develop a strong inner perfectionist, with a focus on great care for details after hours and hours of delayed gratification.

But here too are unintentional consequences. Too much delayed gratification can burn them out and kill their initial motivation, their passion, which is exactly what helped them develop their "future" character in the first place. They tend to become workaholics and burn out.

Further research showed that the healthiest, happiest, highest performers blend the best of both worlds. The quest for the flow state will naturally motivate the "future" toward the hope of an anticipated reward while the "presents" will always be drawn to the pleasure and satisfaction of the present moment. But it is the ones who learn to balance those two worlds that will experience Flow on a more regular basis.

As a society, we have associated becoming an adult with putting aside our natural instincts to play and have fun, in order to achieve peak performances. We forget that "play" is an activity fundamental to our well-being, also tied to the greatest neurochemical rewards the brain can produce, and essential to achieving peak performance and overall satisfaction.

That is why, when I practice, my focus is more on fixing, correcting or tweeking as many details as possible, but when I walk on stage, I forget delay gratification. The public is paying to watch me enjoy what I do, so it is time to eat and enjoy my marshmallow.

**Hard work without talent is a shame,
but talent without hard work is a tragedy.**

Robert Half

CHAPTER 2
LAST-MINUTE TOOLS:
CONCRETE TOOLS
FOR A LAST-MINUTE BOOST

List of tools in this chapter:

A-Tools for physical manifestation (in the body):

1. The Fader technique: 4-4-2
2. Emergency exhale
3. Wake your body: tap, tap, tap
4. Contract/Relax
5. Boost your inner chemistry with power poses

B-Tools for psychological manifestation (in the mind):

6. Smile on cue
7. Gratitude journal
8. Alternate tools for happiness: an email of praise, act of kindness, regular physical activity
9. The power of your words: Change your inner dialogue
10. The art of reframing: "yet", "what if?", "I'm excited" and other last-minute key phrases

Let's imagine that you are just a few minutes away from a performance and I am with you back stage to give you a hand. What can I do to help?

Depending on how you feel I may need to use different strategies. Is the stress running through you so fast that your head is spinning, and you are stuck in worst-case scenarios? Are you feeling paralysed and frozen or are your hands shaking and your body too tense to perform at your best?

No matter how the stress is manifesting itself, I have some great tools for you. Since knowledge is power, let me clarify first what stress is, where does it come from, what is its function, and then we will take action to transform it.

Stress 101

Too often we associate feeling nervous with the idea that something is wrong with us or that something will necessarily go wrong. There is nothing wrong with you, stress is a normal response when you are stepping outside of your zone of comfort.

Before going on stage, or in an audition, it could simply be the signal that your brain is sending you, to remind you that what you are about to do is important to you. That you care and that you really want to give your best. You are simply out of your zone of comfort because you are doing something that you are not used to do.

Many of the activities that make life rewarding, enriching and satisfying also elicit some fear. It's impossible to take risks or face challenges without feeling these feeling.[6]

Stress is not a disease, it is a necessity. It is a survival mechanism. It comes from a primitive programming often called the reptilian brain, vital to ensure our survival. You do not want to get rid of it. Your brain is really trying to help you, to save you by activating a stress response each time it detects a threat.

Stress is generally defined as the automatic response of the brain in the presence of a perceived threat. Perceived is the important word here because it is subjective. That is why some people are nervous on stage and others are not. That response happens when your brain anticipates that the demands necessary to face the challenge exceed your inner resources. Whether the danger is real or not makes no difference. If your brain thinks it is a threat, that fight or flight response is automatically activated.

That response has a physiological effect: the production of hormones (adrenaline and cortisol to name a few) creates rapid heartbeats, sweating, trembling or shaking, dry mouth, shortness of breath and many physical tensions in the body. The other manifestation is psychological: your brain will automatically narrow its focus on the perceived threat to make sure that you are not distracted when facing the "enemy".

If you are in real danger, you will need that rush of adrenaline to take action. You are hardwired biologically to ensure your survival and safety. It is a natural human response.

The twist is that your fear response is very adaptive, because your survival depends on it. Your brain has to learn to recognize danger or threat quickly in order to keep you safe. You will then generalize or associate fear with objects or situations perceived as potentially threatening. That is how we develop an over sensitive alarm system that takes off in situations that are "learned" as dangerous—when in reality it is purely neutral. Exactly

6   Orsillo, Roemer, *Worry Less, Live More*, P.22

like the learned helplessness of the dogs in Seligman's experiment in the introduction.

Our job will be to make a new association. To learn a new habit. The first step will be to calm down the automatic response generated by your sympathetic nervous system (SNS= the system that activates and manages the energy in your body and your fight or flight response). You will use its counterpart as an antidote: the parasympathetic nervous system (PSNS= the one responsible for the recuperation of your energy). Those two systems have an antagonistic function. When one is activated, the other one goes down immediately. Think of it as a seesaw. One side represent the SNS and the other one the PSNS.

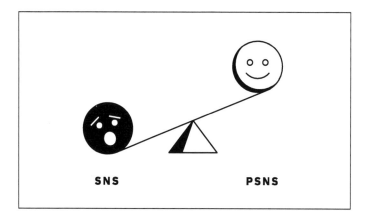

SNS   PSNS

I will show you clever ways to awaken your parasympathetic nervous system on demand. And since we have a physiological and psychological manifestation, I will propose some tools for each one of those two reactions.

> **There is more wisdom in your body than in your deepest philosophy.**
>
> *Friedrich Nietzsche*

A - Tools for Physical Manifestation:

Your secret weapon to counteract the physiological effect of stress is your body. By re-establishing a connection with some specific physical sensations, you will engage your parasympathetic nervous system. That awareness to your body will take you out of your head and will bring you into the present moment. In creating a better link with what is going on in your body, you will be able to awaken your parasympathetic system and lower the effect of your initial stress response.

1. The Fader technique (4-4-2):

To induce a quick relaxation response, very often people use some kind of breathing technique. In emergency situations, when you feel overwhelmed by stress, you need something easy to do and very effective to regain control over your body's autonomous response.

In my workshops, I like to start my last-minute tools with the most spectacular one. The one used in extreme situations by firefighters, SEAL teams and world-class athletes, as proposed by sport psychologist Jonathan Fader.

To activate your parasympathetic nervous system, you need to bring your breathing to approximately six breath per minute. You can achieve this by counting four seconds for each inhalation, four seconds for each exhalation and then a two-seconds pause.

These simple steps, not only bring down your biological alarm response but it also helps you regain a sense of control and inner focus. By giving yourself a concrete task like counting while breathing and being aware of some physical sensations (like the movement of the air in your belly), your racing mind will calm down like a beaming light shining through a cloud of fog. Within seconds, you will experience a sense of clarity and be able to take the actions necessary to perform at your best.

To get the best results, I suggest that you practice this simple exercise in advance. You can incorporate it into your preparation routine: doing it for two or three minutes before you start practicing, or even one minute before each run-through. This exercise or any of the following last-minute tools can be incorporated into your daily routine easily. Take the one that speaks to you the most and use it regularly. That way, when stress arises, you are ready and know what to do.

In summary:

Inhale on a count of four

Exhale on a count of four

Pause for two seconds

2. Emergency exhale

In a high-pressure situation, most of the time, stress will manifest itself by an over-excited state with your thoughts going 100 miles a minute in your head, sweaty palms or cold hands, your body shaking and your heart pumping.

Maybe the stress makes you feel like a garden hose that has many holes in it with the water spilling everywhere except where you need it to go! You need to stop the bleeding.

When you feel over-excited, first you have to get rid of the excess of energy. You can shake your body, jump, run, or shake it. If you are embarrassed, go in a bathroom and shake your arms, your head, your torso and jump a few times.

Then you are ready for the real magic trick: Put one hand on your belly, below your navel, and as you exhale completely push your belly in. It is not a singing exercise, it is a diaphragmatic breathing exercise. You need to go to the complete end of your exhalation. Really push the air completely out. Then you let the air come in and do that sequence another time. In fact, I always suggest to do it three times in a row. Then you will feel your body and your head in a much calmer and focus state.

GRETEL RUNNING A MARATHON:

The night of the Premiere of Hansel and Gretel at l'Opéra de Montréal, Isabelle, a soprano from *l'Atelier lyrique*, was about to make her debut singing Gretel when five minutes before the show she looked at me and said: "There is no way I can sing in this state, I feel like I'm about to explode." Since we had worked together many times in mental preparation for the last two years, I knew her well. So I asked her "what do you need?" She said "I need to get rid of it, to free myself, I need to evacuate this overflow of energy." I said "go for it then." And she ran, in costume, twice back and forth to whole length of the back stage. Still trying to catch her breath two minutes later, smiling, she said "I feel so much better...now I can calm down..." She took her place in the décor as the orchestra started the Overture. And yes, she sang an amazing show.

In summary:

Get rid of the excess energy: jumping, running, shaking your body.
Put your hand below your navel and do three complete and forced exhales in a row.

3. Wake up your body: tap, tap, tap

Sometimes, stress manifests itself in a completely different manner. Have you ever felt tired, drained, with no energy, almost paralysed with an inner dialogue like "I didn't sleep enough, I should have eaten more, I'll never have enough energy to perform"? I have news for you: you are not tired, you are nervous. That under-excitement is just another manifestation of stress and there is an easy way to whip up your energy in two minutes.

With one hand, gently tap the opposite arm from the hand up to the shoulder and return by gently tapping the underside of your arms. You do this back and forth tapping twice on one arm. Switch and do the other arm. Then, you do the same thing for the legs: tap gently, like you were trying to wake up your body, from top to bottom, front and back with one leg twice then the other leg. Continue tapping your buttocks, then your lower back, your belly, your chest and finally with just piano playing fingers on the back of the neck and your head. You'll feel some tingling, like champagne bubbles all over your body. You have just freed yourself from the accumulated surface tension that was holding you back.

Now that you have re-established contact and that your body is awake, you can do the three exhales suggested in the first exercise. You may not feel 100% energic but you will have raised your vital energy from 5% to easily 40 to 50%. With that, you can do yourself justice in your upcoming performance.

In summary:

Gently tap one arm, up and down twice, then the other arm; one leg up and down twice, then the other leg. Gently tap your buttocks, lower back, belly, chest, and finally, piano playing the back of your neck and your head. Then add three complete and forced exhales.

Some eye exercises can also help create openness and calm. When you are stressed, your gaze tends to freeze or become more like a tunnel vision. It is turned inside because of the intense inner dialogue. All you need is to look up and far away, then down, then look from the far right to the far left, and end by making a complete circle, clockwise, then counter clockwise. The effect is subtle, but this exercise facilitates openness and a letting-go in the mind.

Even when you walk on stage, this little eye-gymnastic exercise can have a positive impact for you as well as for the audience. I have noticed that great divas often walk on stage for a recital and look slowly at the whole audience, from one side of the hall to the other. I suspect that this simple gesture (maybe unconscious) not only allows them to establish a warm rapport with the public, but also opens and prepares the inner space needed to reach their zone of excellence.

4. Too tense to perform: Contract/relax

Whether you are over-excited or low energy, you may experience some unwanted tension in your body. Maybe your hands are shaking, maybe your neck is too stiff or maybe you cannot feel your abdomen.

If you are an instrumentalist and part of your body is too stiff or too tight, you will not be able to give your best. If you are a singer, your body is your instrument so it is even more problematic because to resonate optimally, there should be minimal tension in the body.

When your legs or your hands are shaking, it is because they are too tense and you are losing the usual control on those muscles. The best way to reclaim the helm is to do the opposite of what logic dictates. Instead of trying to relax, I encourage you to make it more tense for a few seconds. This idea comes from the Jacobson relaxation technique, (also known as progressive relaxation therapy), often used to help with anxiety.

If your hands are shaking for example, make a fist and squeeze as hard as you can for five seconds, and you can also inhale while you squeeze. Then relax, exhale and do it one more time. Always do it two or three times, fully contracting for five seconds while inhaling, then relax. Try it, you will feel the difference immediately.

You can do it before you walk on stage, and if you are already on stage like an orchestra musician, an oratorio singer or between two pieces, you can use this tool without anyone in the audience noticing that you are doing it. You can squeeze your abdomen, your tongue, even your butt for a few seconds to unlock the accumulated tension. It frees not only your body, it also takes you out of your head.

In summary:

Contract a body part for five seconds while inhaling; then relax, exhale and do it one more time; do this two or three times for each tense body part.

5. Boost your inner chemistry with power poses

It seems there is some truth behind the saying: *Fake it until you make it*. Social psychologist Amy Cuddy demonstrated in her researches that your body language has a direct impact on your emotional state.

She tested the effect of two opposite postures on hormonal production:
A) "High Power Poses", which are usually an expression of openness and expansion (for example, sitting with your feet on your desk and your hands crossed behind your head);

B) "Low Power Poses", which involve folding up and closing your body to make yourself smaller (for example, crossed legs, the chest forward and slumped, arms crossed).

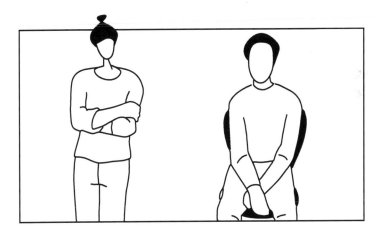

She took measurements of testosterone (the hormone associated with strength and taking action) and cortisol (the hormone that slows down your capacity to react) levels before and after her test subjects held a specific posture for two minutes. She found a 20% increase in testosterone and a 25% decrease in cortisol amongst those who had adopted the high-power postures, while the other group, who were in postures of low power, showed a 10% decrease in testosterone and a 15% increase in cortisol.

This is invaluable information for people preparing for a challenge. If you take a high-power pose and hold it for two minutes, you will provoke within your body a hormonal reaction that will in turn generate an emotional state that corresponds to this posture. In taking a posture of power, you have a better chance of feeling powerful and self-confident.

It is possible that you worry about the authenticity of that inner state: you may be afraid of being artificial or being seen as an impostor because you do not feel it inside of you. In her famous TED talk, Amy Cuddy's conclusion proposed that if you pretend and keep on pretending (because what you are doing is really important to you), it can not only succeed, but can also transform permanently your performance. It transforms the saying "fake it until you make it" into "fake it until you become it"!

If you think about it, that is exactly how children learn. They have fun pretending to do something until the experience is assimilated, and they can make this new behaviour their own.

In summary:
Take a high-power pose and hold it for two minutes.

THE RACHMANINOV PIANO CONCERTO

Back in the 1980s when I was a young pianist at the beginning of my career, I had the chance to go on a number of tours. During one of these tours with the *Orchestre des Jeunes du Québec* (Québec Youth Orchestra), just before the third night in a row of playing Rachmaninov's Second Piano Concerto in different cities, I was suddenly afraid that I would not have enough energy to get through the performance. Fatigue (or was it stress disguised as fatigue?) meant that I had to use a different approach.

A few days before going on tour, I saw a documentary about Arthur Rubenstein in concert. His authority, his calm, the magnitude of his performance, and especially, his posture at the piano inspired me. His back was so straight that it was almost curved backwards, his gaze was high and went off into the distance instead of being fixed on the keyboard.

Just before going out on stage, I had a crazy idea: To reassure the public and to at least put on a good show, I decided to pretend to be a great pianist like Arthur Rubenstein. I adopted a posture "à la Rubinstein," and started. After a few pages—just a few minutes of pretending—all my energy was back and the pleasure of playing carried me through the end of the concerto. I did not have a logical explanation at that time, but now I understand much better what helped me. I pretended to be calm and at ease until I really was. To be precise, by pretending, I was able to return to the state of confidence and pleasure that I had known a number of times during rehearsal.

B - Tools for Psychological manifestation:

Your brain function is at its best when you are happy!

Positive psychology has demonstrated through much research that the brain functions optimally when we are happy, not when negative or neutral. When we are happy, our brain produces hormones (dopamine and serotonin among others) that not only make us feel good but actually facilitate our learning process and our ability to make more connections.

It sometime feels as if we were born to be negative. And I would say it is partly right—it is an evolutionary trait. It is part of our survival mechanism. It is normal to be on the look-out, to be vigilant about the dangers that can present themselves... but only to a certain point...

People are afraid that if they are happy, they will not fix their problems. We do not realize that when we buy into the idea that fear is a great motivator, we activate our fight or flight response, which is more of a last resort solution—very short term and not something to help us thrive.

When we engage in an activity that we feel passionate about, that we love, the hormones that our brain produces will broaden the amount of possibilities we can process, making us more creative and more open to new connexions.

A NIGHT AT THE OPÉRA:

I was back stage at the second show of the opera Fedora in which I was playing the role of Lazinsky, a pianist invited to the ball of the second act and who plays a solo piece in the middle of the act. I was about the make my entrance with my "date", Anne, the young soprano in that show. She was so relaxed, smiling, comfortable while I was very nervous. I asked her: "How do you stay so cool? You seem exactly the same as in rehearsals, just yourself, aren't you nervous?" She answered smiling, "well, to be honest, I realized a few years ago that when I'm not singing at my best, I sing at about 75% of my capacity.

At 75% of my potential, there might be two people in the 3000 present that can really tell the difference. Am I going to ruin my pleasure of singing because maybe two persons will be able to tell that I'm not at 100% ? I chose to sing because I love it and I do it the best I can each night. That's all I can do."

> ## Happiness is the joy you feel while working towards your potential.
>
> *Shawn Achor*

But can we practice being happy? Is it a crazy idea?

6. Smile on cue

Several years ago, I took a workshop on stress management with an expert named Cecilia. I had never seen or met her before. When I saw her preparing before the class, she looked very serious, driven and borderline bossy. Just before going in front of the 40 people present for the workshop, she smiled as she walked in front of the class and looked at everybody before starting to talk. Yes, she was a beautiful woman, but that smile could have melted any iceberg. It was so powerful that within five seconds, the whole group was under her spell. The transformation from serious to irradiating happiness, joy and authenticity inspired me.

What could I do to have more of what she had? Could I practice channeling that inner state on demand? I had this crazy idea that maybe if I practice smiling, genuinely and authentically, I could improve my presence and add more warmth to my presence so I can tap into it at will.

I was not sure it would work, and I felt a little silly, but two or three times a day, whenever I felt neither negative nor positive, I chose consciously to practice smiling. I would think of a funny joke, a funny video I saw or the memory of Cecilia at the beginning of the workshop and boom, I would start to radiate a warm and happy inner state.

The secret is to practice it when you feel good or neutral. Not as an escape to avoid feeling sad or afraid. Just a little kick toward a more positive feeling and hold it only for two or three seconds. When you leave your house and you lock the door, when you wait for the subway or before you start practicing your instrument, tune into a "happy channel" for a few seconds.

A little trick I often use is to start with the opposite of a smile. Instead of starting from neutral, I contact a feeling of being very serious, annoyed, or a little exasperated then gradually I bring a smile and go as full and as warm as possible without losing my authenticity. The contrast makes it even more fun to experience. It is extremely addictive because you will enjoy feeling good and you will want more.

In summary:
Choose an image or a memory that brings a smile to your face easily, like the memory of a baby smiling, of a puppy, of a good joke you heard or some TV bloopers, and from a neutral state bring in the most authentic and radiant smile you can for two or three seconds.

> **"A smile costs nothing but creates much. It enriches those who receive it, without impoverishing those who give it. It happens in a flash and the memory of it sometimes lasts forever. No one is rich enough to do without."**
>
> *Dale Carnegie*

7. Gratitude diary

To help you cultivate a more positive outlook on life, or if you tend to be an over active pessimist, here is an excellent exercise that can make a big difference:

In his book *Happier: Learn the Secrets to Daily Joy and Lasting Fulfilment*, positive psychologist Tal Ben- Shahar shares with his readers the content of a class on happiness he taught at Harvard University. Among other things, he asked his students to keep a gratitude diary for the duration of the course, because as he explained, cultivating thankfulness every day is one of the keys to achieve happiness.

Each day, the students write in their diaries three to five things they are thankful for. It can be something they did, something they experienced, or simply something they are thankful to have present in their lives. It is an excellent way to end the day. Instead of rehashing everything that torments you, you can look at yourselves and your day with kindness. It is like an automatic letting-go that happens on its own when you choose to direct your attention towards what you appreciate in life.

In the last ten years, there have been so many studies and reports from scientists demonstrating the positive effects of a regular gratitude practice. They show the impact on hormone production in the mind and the general wellbeing of the test subjects who went through this simple process.

I encourage you to take the two-week challenge and keep a gratitude diary and see for yourself the effect that it has. It is the tool I receive the most positive feedback for on a regular basis. Personally, I started with writing three things and after a few weeks, because it is so addictive, I ended up using five or six phrases every night. You write the "what and the why": what happen that made you happy, that you are grateful for—and why. Here is an example of the form it can take:

Friday, July 24th. I am so thankful:
For having slept so well, so easily, so deeply, and to wake up refreshed.

For being in great shape, in good health and to have taken the time to go to the gym, it made me feel so good after.

For the incredible opportunity to be in Berlin and to share what I am passionate about. It felt like I'm at my place.

For the conversation with my friend Marie that made me laugh so much.

For the email this afternoon asking me to give another workshop in the fall, it was exciting and gave me a wonderful sense of recognition.

If you choose to do it before going to bed, it will help you put on positive glasses before you fall asleep, which is a great strategy to improve your sleeping habits.

If you prefer to start your day with it, go ahead. There is no wrong way of doing this.

Those who do not like to write can do it while brushing their teeth. An excellent strategy is to use a regular habit that you already have and to attach a new one like this gratitude praise.

Some have decided to start the family evening dinner with everybody sharing one thing they are happy with that happened during their day. Have fun with it and adapt it to fit into your lifestyle.

If you have a tendency to be overly negative and always focus on what does not go your way, maybe you can get inspiration from the best strategy to use when a child is throwing a tantrum. The advice of professionals is to ignore them when they are acting out and congratulate them when they do the desire behaviour. As science has proven many times, they will do more and more of the rewarded behaviour. You can think of it as a way to develop the habit of celebrating your small wins, which will have a major impact on your motivation and on your drive to succeed. For us musicians, because we tend to be perfectionists and future-oriented, this new habit of taking time for gratitude—to recognize our little victories—will go a long way in building confidence.

As far as last-minute tools are concerned, to connect with the feeling of gratitude is an excellent antidote because it is incompatible with stress. You cannot feel fear and gratitude at the same time. That means that if you take time to revisit a memory of something you feel grateful for or just think about what you are grateful for in your life, you will activate your parasympathetic nervous system and lower your stress level immediately.

In summary:
Write three to five things that you are grateful for, take time to write **what** happened and **why** you are thankful for it.

8. A few suggestions as alternative tools for happiness
Psychologist and author of *The Happiness Advantage*, Shawn Achor, proposed a few more tools to build your happiness by very small steps each day. Since happiness is subjective and different for everyone, take time to explore and figure out what works best for you.

Start your day with writing a short email, just a few lines to thank or praise someone. It will activate the hormone production of serotonin and dopamine that will give you a quick boost of positive emotions, improving your focus and general well-being.

Carry out a conscious act of kindness like giving your seat to someone in the bus, opening the door for someone, letting a pedestrian or a car go first etc. Deliberate and conscious action is an important criterion in achieving best results.

Some studies were done to test the impact of acts of altruism and demonstrated that when individuals completed five acts of kindness during the course of a day, they felt much happier than the control group and that feeling lasted for several days.

Engage in regular physical activity. One element that I always forget to mention is the importance of regular physical activity. Probably because it has always been a part of my daily life, I tend to assume that everybody knows that exercising is not only a powerful mood-lifter but also a long-lasting one. Exercising releases pleasure-inducing chemicals called endorphins that can boost your mood, reduce stress and anxiety and help you get into the flow.

In *High Performance Habits*, Brendon Burchard mentions that high performers have more energy and must spend time regularly generating that amazing fuel. He says: *Energy is physical, emotional, and mental—and exercise improves each category.*

I heard conductor Yannick Nezet-Seguin in an interview recently mentioning the importance of his gym workouts in order to maintain his energy and good spirit to face his very challenging schedule. Whether you like to walk, run, bike, play a team sport or go to the gym, chose a sport that you like and just keep moving regularly.

In summary:
Start your day with writing a short email to thank or praise someone,
Carry out a conscious act of kindness,
Engage in regular, physical activity.

9. The Power of Your Words: Change your inner dialogue

Did you know that what you tell yourself just before you go on stage or into an audition room has a major impact on your energy? I often hear singers in the hallway just before an audition mentioning how much they hate auditioning. Although it is an authentic statement of their experience, it is definitely not the best moment to bring it up.

Let me share with you the exercise I use in my workshops to help the participants experience the different effects of a positive versus a negative inner dialogue.

Here is an example of this exercise with singers:

Close your eyes and bring one arm up, parallel to the floor. You resist while I apply pressure to bring it down. It is just as a test for you to feel the amount of strength you need to keep your arm strait.

First part: Keeping your eyes closed, think of a performance that went very well for you and that was really satisfying. Then repeat slowly after me: I love to sing.... it makes me feel amazing to sing.... it fills me with joy and a sense of fulfilment when I sing...

Then put your arms in front of you and resist again while I apply pressure. It is usually even easier than the first time, as if you were having a nice boost of energy.

Second part: close your eyes again and think of a performance that did not go well and that was frustrating or discouraging. Then repeat after me: it is hard to sing... I hate singing in auditions... it makes me feel horrible and empty when I sing in auditions.... put your arm up again and resist. Most people have much less strength to resist or sometimes they can resist but it cost them a lot more energy to keep their arm strait up.

Third part: close your eyes and repeat: I love auditions... I feel amazing when I sing in front of a jury... It fills me with great pleasure each time I sing in an audition. Bring your arm up and resist one last time. Here the strange thing is that even if it is a lie, most people have more strength to resist than after saying the negative (and true) statements.

What is the conclusion we can draw from this little experiment? The words we tell ourselves have an immediate and short-term impact on your physical energy. Even if those words are not true. I am not suggesting that you try to convince yourself by blindly repeating an affirmation that you know is not true. I propose that you bring your focus on what you love, what you are passionate about in that activity. For example, you do not love auditions, but you love to sing... so use: I love to sing. Put the jury and the audition aside for a moment, and focus on why you sing and all the good feelings singing awakens in you.

In summary:

What do you choose to focus on just before a performance or audition?

What will you remind yourself of?

Feel free to mix and use all of these tools to fit your own need of the moment. You may want to do a few in sequence or all at the same time: take a power pose while you do three complete exhale and repeat your favorite positive affirmation in your head a few times. Explore and figure out what your best options are.

SING FOR THE LORD!

Patricia had an exceptional voice and an extraordinary emotional connection with music. She also had a fragile and anxious temperament. It is probably this fragility, this vulnerability, that made her performances so moving. She entered many competitions and she would get extremely nervous. In those times, before going on stage, she would surrender to a force bigger than herself. A strong religious believer, she would simply say, "You gave me this voice... I can't do it alone. You are going to sing through me, I'll let you do it." She would then walk on stage, radiating calm and focus, and she won nearly every competition in which she participated.

10. The art of reframing

Being nervous before or during a performance is totally normal. But the meaning that you give to your stress will make all the difference. If you think that being nervous is the worst thing in the world or a sign that things will go badly, fear will take up more and more space within you. As I mentioned before, your body will react to this alarm by producing, among other things, cortisol (the hormone that slows down your capacity to adequately react) and adrenaline (the "warrior" hormone that pushes you to take action).

When you succeed in changing your perception of a stressful event and see it as a challenge instead of a catastrophe or a danger, your body modifies the production of hormones, decreasing the amount of cortisol in the system, which facilitate the access to your inner resources and allows you to focus your attention on facing this challenge.

He who masters his perceptions, masters life.
Anonymous

If I placed a narrow, two-metre-long plank on the ground and asked you to walk on it, you would do it without hesitating. If I put it on two big beams that lifted it two metres above the ground, most of you would hesitate.

Making music by yourself is one thing but performing in public is another matter. You are about to do something in front of an audience that you can do very well alone, when practicing. All of a sudden, in front of the public and under pressure, you become extremely self-conscious of everything you are doing. It is like walking on a plank above a cliff. The art of reframing is putting the plank back on the ground... in your mind!

The meaning you attach to what happens to you, creates an emotional response. This inner state will be altered according to what you include in your point of view, and what you exclude from it. Just like a photographer who decides how to frame a picture: he determines what will grab your attention in the picture. When you realize that you can change the frame of your perceptions by updating your reference grid with new information, you have access to a greater number of options. And the more options you have (like the ones I propose in this book), the freer you are to choose the direction you want.

You can therefore transform your inner state by changing the frame of reference and give a new meaning to what happens to you. It can be as simple as changing a phrase like "I can't do it," to "I can't do it *yet*."

Add "yet"

This is one of the first reframing games that I experienced many years ago. You take negative phrases such as:

- I can't...
- I'm not able to...
- It's impossible for me to...

And you reformulate them, adding the word "yet." For example:

- I can't .... yet.
- I'm not able to....... yet...
- It's impossible for me to...yet.

Change the negative phrases that you regularly use, and stay open to the new possibility, even if you do not believe it...yet! In order to change a belief, you need to first create a doubt in your mind. Remember:
Meaning is not something we find, but something that we give.

In summary:

Use a limiting negative phrase you tell yourself and add "yet" at the end.

What if....

Perhaps you have experienced something difficult in the past, an event that seemed to be the worst thing that could possibly happen to you. Then you discovered, a few months later, that it was actually the turning point that allowed you to begin a very positive transformation. It could be, for example, the loss of a job that allowed you to find another one that is clearly better for you, and beyond what you could have imagined. Or perhaps a mistake that led you to discover a path that you never would have followed otherwise.

To create a doubt in your mind, all you have to do is recall a concrete example like the one I just mentioned, taken from your personal experience. You can then use this example during hard times and tell yourself, "What if what I am experiencing now was to ultimately bring something wonderful and unexpected, like the time that..."

In this way, you can modify your frame of reference by including this new data that changes your perception. The certainty of your first perception is shaken and called into question by this realization that opens up all kinds of new possibilities.

I'm excited!

Physiologically, anxiety and excitement feel the same in your body. It is the exact same thing, the only difference is what your mind calls it—the story you tell yourself, the narrative you resort to automatically. The reframing does not stop the feeling surging through your body. It just gives your mind an explanation that empowers you and then the feeling does not escalate.

DO YOU LIKE HORROR MOVIES?

I was working with Alexis, an excellent baritone, who was feeling stressed out the night before an important audition. I asked him to describe the physical manifestation of his stress related to his audition. He said, "I am overexcited, my hands tremble, I can't stay still, I get butterflies in my stomach, my thoughts bounce around in my mind at high speed."

I asked him what situation other than an audition or a concert had caused those same sensations in the past. After thinking for a moment, he said, "just before jumping when I used to do bungee jumping! I would be excited and afraid at the same time. I know that I want to do it, I know that it will be exhilarating, but I'm still terrified."

"What makes you jump instead of giving in to fear?" I asked him since the two situations seemed to be very similar in terms of the physical sensations he experienced. "I keep my attention on the excitement and the rush that the jump will give me, and not on the fear," he said spontaneously. Then, after a few moments of reflection, he concluded, "I could really do the same with the audition, and say to myself just before going in, 'it's like a bungee jump, go ahead, jump! Focus on the excitement!'"

It is sort of the same thing that happens whenever we watch a horror film: we are afraid, and we like it... but we do not like auditions...strange, no?

IT'S CHRISTMAS

The morning of an important Gala, Ingrid, one of my good friends, was so worried that she constantly repeated, "I'm too nervous, way too nervous, I'm worried that I'll need more

Immodium." In a moment of clarity, she remembered our previous conversation about reframing so she stopped and analysed her reaction, then asked herself how she could reformulate it: What other words could I use instead of "I'm nervous?" How could I say the same thing in a more positive, stimulating way?

She took the time to play with that idea and one memory came to her: "I'm as excited as when I was five years old on Christmas Eve, just before opening my presents. It's the same level of energy in my body. I feel stimulated and authentic when I say to myself, "I'm excited, and I will put that energy at the service of everything I do during the concert." By changing the way she formulated her stress, turning it into an empowering mantra, she was able to give a performance that to this day still serves her as an inspiration when she feels the pressure rising.

A journalist once asked the rock singer Bruce Springsteen if he was still nervous before going on stage after so many years of concerts in front of crowds of 50, 000 people. He answered, "Never. When I get ready to go on stage, my heart starts pounding, my hands start shaking, my breath goes up into my throat, and I know I am pumped and ready to play."

Paul McKenna [7]

Last-Minute Key Phrases

Most performers, whether artists or athletes, have expressions that they really like to remind themselves of to reduce the pressure just before starting. It helps them reconnect with their deepest motivation. It is a short phrase that brings them back down to earth.

If you are looking for inspiration, here are a few examples:

I didn't pick this career to suffer.

At the end of the day, it's only "show business."

It's not brain surgery, nobody is going to die tonight.

---

7   Paul McKenna, I Can Make You Confident, P.205

> **It's not the end of the world. My dog will still lick**
> **my face when I come home whether I win or lose.**
>
> *Matt Biondi, Olympic swimmer*

Maybe you have one similar phrase that you like to repeat to yourself?

In summary:
Prepare a couple of phrases in advance, write them down and bring them with you backstage to remind you of the meaning you give to this upcoming challenge.

I'M SEXY….

During a Masterclass with the singers of the Atelier lyrique of the Montreal Opera, Sophia, who had just done brilliantly at an important audition a few weeks before, performed with unusual ease and fire. Curious, I asked her what had allowed her to sing with so much pleasure and fluidity.

She turned red, smiled, and looking a little embarrassed, admitted that at her last audition, what had made all the difference was that just before singing, she said to herself, "I'm sexy and I have lots of friends." It completely freed her. All the singers burst out laughing and admitted that Sophia had put her finger on something powerful. Was it the fear of rejection that had dissolved? Or the fear of not being loved that all of a sudden did not have any hold on her anymore? She followed her instinct and adopted this new mantra that led her to success.

> **You don't have to see the whole**
> **staircase, just take the first step.**
>
> *Martin Luther King*

CHAPTER 3
WHAT IS YOUR GOAL?

List of tools in this chapter:

<u>A - Long term goal:</u>
1. The Ladder

<u>B-Goals of action</u>
2. The Road or the Cliff?
3. The Pyramid of a musician (outer game)
4. Implantation of Intention

<u>C-Short term goal for today's performance</u>
5. Your short-term goal
6. Suggestions for final formulation
7. Bonus material: three criteria

**The bow and the arrow.
You might be an excellent archer, but if there is no
target in front you, it is impossible to shoot your arrow
in the right direction.... Most of the time, we are stuck
in life simply because we don't carry within us the direction
that our deepest mind must follow.**

Olivier Lockert [8]

The million-dollar question, the most important one to ask yourself (and not just in the context of a performance) is: "What do I want?" or if you prefer, "What is my goal?"

8 Translated from : Olivier Lockert, *Confiance et estime de soi avec l'hypnose*, P.27

It's the question I ask myself every week, sometimes even several times a day. Am I really going where I want to go, or am I letting life decide for me? Clarifying this question allows me to line up the inner resources of the unconscious mind with my actions, helping me reach my goal quickly and easily.

Do you remember Alice in Wonderland when she arrived at the cross roads and asked the Cheshire Cat anxiously:

Would you tell me, please, which way I ought to go from here?

The Cheshire Cat: That depends a good deal on where you want to get to.

Alice: I don't much care where.

The Cheshire Cat: Then it doesn't much matter which way you go.

Alice: ...So long as I get somewhere.

The Cheshire Cat: Oh, you're sure to do that, if only you walk long enough."

Do you really know what you want or are you like a boat going along with the flow of the sea? Or maybe you know what you do not want any more, but have no idea what exactly you want instead. Studies in psychology have demonstrated that the most important aspect to explore in order to maximize your chances of reaching a goal is to build a clear mental representation of what you want. Not how you will get there but the end results you are after. Your brain will then activate his search engine to capture all the possibilities that will present themselves to help you reach that goal.

Over the years, I realized that clarifying what you want as a performer will benefit you more when you delve into it from three different perspectives: long term goal, short term goal and goals of action during your performance. Each of these goals carries many helpful elements that will change the way you perform.

A - Long term goal:

The first thing to shed light on is: What drives you? What makes you so passionate about music? Why do you play your instrument? Why do you sing?

I have a very easy and simple exercise that will help you uncover your inner motivation. That information will be your greatest asset to disarm your fears when you're under pressure.

It has been demonstrated many times that external motivation, like a reward or avoiding a punishment, will not be your best source of motivation to give a great performance. Internal motivation, also call intrinsic motivation, is associated with the enjoyment that your activity brings you and the pleasure of getting better at this activity. When your mind is too focussed on the external reward or on the end game, you fail to connect with your deepest driving force, and you cannot access the selfless state of the Flow necessary to free your full potential.

1. The Ladder

I called this exercise the Ladder, as an analogy of going up or maybe more accurately going down deeper into your inner world of motivation. Each step will bring important information to help you build a clearer links with your own inner drive to play or sing.

First step:
A - How would you define your ability?
What is "singing" or "playing the piano/violin/etc." for you?

There are no right or wrong answers here. For some people it is telling a story, for someone else it is connecting with people; it can be expressing yourself or releasing emotions or healing people through the music or sharing who you really are. Take time to figure out what your personal connection is.

If you are not sure, that is totally normal. Let the question find its way inside you. Maybe several answers will come up later today or tomorrow. You will write it down then.
B - How would you define making music?
Now let us focus more specifically on the sound aspect. Sometimes, singers will describe singing more in terms connected with acting or theater. Here I want to bring out your connection with music. If it is your case, why music and not acting for example? If you are an instrumentalist, what does "making music" mean for you?

Maybe your answer is similar to the way you defined singing or playing your instrument. Or maybe you uncover new elements like: you mold sounds like a sculptor, or you juggle with sounds to create emotional images, or maybe it is about a connection with your soul. Let your imagination guide you and write down everything that comes up.

Second step:
Why do you sing?
Why do you play the piano/violin/your instrument?
What does "singing" or "playing your instrument" bring you?
Most likely, it is because you love it. Then what do you love about it more specifically?

Is it the sound making process that makes you feel like a magician or a juggler?

Is it the connection with the composer?

The sharing and honoring his master piece?

Is it the physical aspect of what it makes you feel when you sing or play?

Is it the emotional journey that it brings you each time?

Is it the connection with others: the public or the colleagues with whom you sing or play?

It nourishes what in you?

Does it feed a need to...?

Third step:

Let's dig a little deeper and for each answer of the second step ask:

In what way is... (ex: expressing who you are) important for you?

Or what does... (expressing who you are) bring you?

Maybe it makes you feel alive, completed, free, connected to your own power, connected to a force bigger than you. Just trust what comes up for you.

Fourth step:

When you were younger, what attracted you to singing or playing your instrument?

How did it all begin?

What was the determining factor?

Was it a revelation or something that build up over several encounters?

If that is the case, when did you finally choose this path and what made you decide to pursue it?

Did someone special inspire you? If so, in what way?

Often, revisiting your roots, your own unique story will bring out some meaningful insight.

Last step:

After all those questions and answers, now you are ready to choose two or three elements that really resonate in you. They will help you reconnect and remind you of your own personal values in strategic moments (like just before you go on stage, or the day after a troublesome performance).

> **Before each important activity, meeting, or event, athletes I work with will go through a routine in which they remind themselves to "put the ME into it". The M stands for Motivation and the E stands for Enjoyment.**
>
> *Jonathan Fader* [9]

In summary:

First step:

a - How would you define your ability?

What is singing or playing the violin for you?

b - Then: How would you define making music?

—

Second step:

Why do you sing?

Why do you play the piano/violin/your instrument?

What does singing or playing your instrument bring you?

What do you love about it specifically?

—

Third step:

In what way is... (ex: expressing who you are) important for you?

Or what does... (ex: expressing who you are) bring you?

—

Fourth step:

When you were younger, what attracted you to singing or playing your instrument?

How did it all begin?

What was the determinant factor? (deciding factor)

—

Last step:

Choose two or three elements that really resonate in you.

9   Jonathan Fader, *Life as Sport*, P.8

A word of wisdom: You are more than what you do!

Maybe you have been singing or playing your instrument for enough years now that you actually identify yourself as a singer or as a violinist, pianist etc. I cannot remember when exactly the switch happened for me but somewhere in my twenties, I started to refer to myself as a pianist. If someone asked me "who are you?" I would say, "I'm Claude Webster, pianist." There is a catch to that feeling of identification that is important to be aware of.

Harmonious Passion versus Obsessive Passion

The concept of passion for an activity is defined in psychology as a strong inclination towards a self-defining activity that people love, to which they devote a significant amount of time and energy. That activity may become a central part of a person's identity. For example, someone who is passionate about playing the violin may consider themselves a violinist—it defines who he or she is.

In harmonious passion, *a person freely chooses to engage in an activity for the pleasure derived from it, without external or internal pressure.* [10] It is characterized by a flexibility that leaves space for other important aspect of their life.

Obsessive passion on the other hand, happens when a person is controlled by external (acceptance from peers or teachers) or internal pressure. It then creates conflicts with other parts of their lives.

We all wish to be inhabited by harmonious passion because it helps us remain the captain of our ship. The best advice I received in that department was to make the difference between "who I am" and "what I do".

Olympic acrobatic skier Alexandre Bilodeau, after his first appearance at the Olympics, worked with a sport psychologist to prepare for his next competitions. Interestingly, the first thing his psychologist did was help him redefine himself. Alexandre explained in an interview that "before I was an acrobatic skier, now I'm Alex and skiing is my passion."

You are more than what you do. You are worth more than how you played or sang today.

You are not worth less because you did not win first prize. That subtle separation will help you find a balance between what you do and who you are. Honour what you do, the form in which you have found and chosen to express your passion and your uniqueness.

Let us imagine that what you do is like a horizontal plane. You tend to identify with your past, and the now is too often a means to an end—to build your future. Then you also have a vertical dimension to your being. A plane that represents your true self, the

---

10   Bonneville-Roussy, Lavigne and Vallerand, *When Passion Leads to Excellence, the case of musicians.*

one free from your accomplishments. Who you are is probably better represented by the vertical dimension and then, you express who you are through the horizontal plane.

To know yourself better, is to know why you do what you do and at the same time, know that you are more than what you are doing.

B - Goals of Action

For some musicians, just clarifying their goals of action, the step by step operating instructions and the constant readjustments, will be enough to counter-act their stress. They will still feel nervous, but it will not matter because they know what to do and they are too busy doing it to worry about anything else. Those actions are what I call the outer game.

This section will show you many suggestions to build your operating map in a very conscious and effective way. It will allow you to stay in the "now" during your performance. When you are in the Flow, the effortless characteristic is linked with having very clear goals, feedback and readjustments necessary to stay aligned with those goals.

First, I need to guide you through the key concept of the goal formulation: the road or the cliff. Then, I will introduce my version of all the elements necessary for a classical musician to juggle when making music with the Pyramid of The Musician. And finally, I will come back with a plan to address your inner game (psychological interferences) through your goals of action with the creation of an intention map.

2. The Road or the Cliff?

I would like to introduce a concept that is at once simple and powerful. If I had to pick one idea that I would like you to keep in mind and use after having read this book, an idea capable of making a difference in your life, it would be this one: the brain cannot produce an inner representation of a negative.

If I said to you, for example, "don't think about Bugs Bunny," your brain will immediately imagine Bugs Bunny. To be more precise, the brain *can* make a representation of a negative, but in two steps. First, it will automatically manifest what was articulated, and then find a way to respond to the negation by creating a new thought.

If I asked you to think about a man not driving a car, you will probably imagine a man and a car, and then choose, for example, to think about a man walking, riding a bicycle or something like that. In the context of a performance, you do not have the time to go through all this process.

This "positive thinking" to obtain better results has nothing to do with a New Age philosophy, or with being a good person; it is simply the way the brain works best. To use a positive formulation is to clearly tell your brain where you want to go.

Imagine that you are driving a car along a winding road along a cliff. If, on top of that, the narrow road is making you nervous, will you keep your eyes on the road, or the cliff? "Keep your eyes on the road!" I hear my driving instructor screaming.

Experience has taught me that if I see something interesting or beautiful while driving, I will automatically go in that direction. So, if I am afraid of falling off the cliff, I better keep my eyes on the road, because what I look for, I will find.

If you wake up in the morning and say to yourself, "I wonder what difficulties I'll run into today?", all your attention will be focused on everything that could confirm that things will go wrong. If, on the contrary, you wake up and tell yourself, "I can't wait to discover what beautiful surprises life will send me today!", you will be open and looking for happy surprises. And since you are looking for them, even if they are very small, you will catch them.

During your performance, is your attention focused on what you do not want, or what you really do want? What does the little voice in your head say during your performance? If you are telling yourself "don't look down", your brain focuses on looking down.

Are you saying to yourself: "Don't rush!" or "Breathe and take your time"? "Stop pushing!" or "Steady and easy?" If you are in the habit of talking to yourself in negative phrases, you lose precious time and are being too vague about what you are hoping to achieve. Your attention is fixed on *not* doing something rather than going ahead directly. It is as if you are driving your car with a foot on the brake.

DO NOT THINK OF NUMBER TWELVE

A few years ago, I was giving a workshop in Tel Aviv on performance preparation and I decided to play a game with the singers. I first asked them to write down all the obligations and orders that usually come to their minds when they sing. Second, they had to find a positive version of all the phrases expressed that contained a negation. For example, "don't slouch," might become, "tall and proud"; "don't be tense," might become "open and relaxed," etc.

To illustrate this concept, I used the following example: "Don't think of the number 12." Every thirty seconds, I repeated, "Whatever you do, don't think about the number 12, don't imagine a black circle with the number 12 written in red inside it!" It was ridiculous, and they laughed heartily, but they also realized that too often, that is exactly what they were doing without realizing it.

The next day, Sara, a young soprano, told me what happened to her during the concert that followed our class. During the musical interlude of one of the arias she was singing, she realized that since the beginning of her aria, she had been repeating interiorly "don't push, don't push."

"Don't think about the number 12" immediately came into her mind. She said to herself "Okay, what's the opposite of pushing for me?" The phrase "bounce like you were sitting on a gym ball" came to her. Her performance changed immediately, becoming more stimulating and satisfying. She had the impression of lifting her foot off the brake and becoming proactive and centred on an action (like bouncing) instead of behaving like a police officer looking for infractions. Even if her performance was not entirely to her liking, her pleasure and satisfaction were so obvious that even her colleagues remarked that the second part of her aria was much more inspired.

THE ROAD OR THE CLIFF IN ACTION:

Now is the time to update the key words of your performance, that is to say, the inner directives that you are going to give yourself while performing.

For many musicians, a common fear is to play wrong notes. If you are afraid of wrong notes or of making a mistake and are focussed on that idea, the better part of your attention is spent observing yourself and holding yourself back. You have to transform this order into something positive.

When you are not afraid of playing a wrong note, what are you focusing on? For you, what is the opposite of making a mistake? There is not a universally-effective solution that everyone can use. The goal is to find the wording that is appropriate for you, and that awakens the motivation to be pro-active instead of over-checking yourself.

Maybe for you it becomes "I play with confidence and freedom." Or "I am playing with sounds." Or "I'll just go for it, no matter how I feel." Or "I connect with the direction of the phrases." Or "My movements are free and confident." Or "I focus on the best possible quality of sound."

Often, people are so obsessed by the problem that they become fixated on it. Singers sometimes tell me, "My problem is my tongue. It is so rigid and tense that I can't free myself up." If they remain concentrated on their tense tongue, they are going straight into the cliff. Muscular tensions are usually better resolved by tensing them for a few seconds and then enjoy the feeling of relaxation as seen in the last-minute tool: contract/relax.

What kind of bench mark will allow you to stay on the road? What phrases or key words do you tell yourself while performing? Do they take the form of actions to be carried out or avoided? A state of mind to escape or produce? What do you tend to say to yourself when things do not go according to plan?

First, write everything that comes up without censuring yourself. Write down all the phrases and words that you tell yourself while you are performing. If the expressions or phrases are negative, be sure to write them down, too. They contain precious information that could ensure the success of your performance. The message is merely incomplete.

All you have to do is transform that message by finding the positive formulation. There is no pre-established miracle solution. Take the time to find the most useful formula. You will know that you have found the right one when it resonates within you, something will light up and fill you with energy.

In summary:

My Cliff (my negative tendencies)	**My Road** (positive direction)
_____	_____
_____	_____
_____	_____

One day, I asked the singers to do this exercise at the end of the first day of a workshop. At the end, Catherine, a soprano, realized that she had written down only positive phrases but that was not at all what she was actually saying to herself during a performance. It was rather what she *should* have said. All the things she knew she *should* have done. The things she tells her students to do. But this is not what she did when under pressure. So, I asked her "What do you really tell yourself?" Then, she began clarifying what I call her tendencies. Some people have a tendency to hold back, some to freeze, others to push. When nervous, we all have a way of behaving that we resort to most often.

This tendency is your cliff. In clearly identifying your cliff, you can quickly notice when your eyes have left your road during your performance and immediately return to it.

If what comes to you spontaneously is, like Catherine, everything that would be ideal to experience in a performance situation, great. That is your road. What is left is to find your cliff. That way, when in a stressful situation you will be able to wake up and recognize the tendencies that may lead you into a ravine rather than staying on the road.

These two pieces of information—your road and your cliff—are the basis of the success of your performance. If it is a sunny day when everything flows easily, you will know the road and follow it with pleasure. If it is a rainy day and there are all sorts of interferences in your head, you will notice it immediately. It is the cliff that you have just clarified. And what do you do when driving next to a cliff? You keep your eyes on the road. And now you have your list of key words to stay in your inner zone of excellence.

3. Pyramid of The Singer or The Instrumentalist = your outer game

Now that you have done a first draft of your performance preparation, I will share with you my version of all the necessary actions that a musician needs to master in order to give an optimal performance. Then, we will put all those elements in a more elaborate exercise to help you build an exhaustive and effective map of actions.

Mastery of such an ability like playing a musical instrument or singing requires a high level of automatization. Like driving a car. At the beginning, it takes lots of concentration and gradually, it becomes more and more fluid. Usually to the point that you feel that driving is easy and you do almost nothing.

You want to experience the same thing with your musical performance. You have programed many *automatisms* that will be executed with a minimum of energy; with just enough consciousness to keep you on the right track and enough awareness left to view the whole process, while keeping all the necessary balls in the air. Do not mistake the *automatisms* necessary to perform your instrument with the automatic pilot which would be a form of avoidance as when your fingers are playing but you are no longer present at the helm.

Let's look at the *automatisms* needed to execute all the right notes. It takes hours and hours of repetition to internalize that information in a way that can be accessed easily and fluidly. And that is only a small part of your job as a musician. Your goal in a performance is not, like children learning an instrument sometimes think, an obstacle course where your focus is to go as quickly as possible hitting all the right notes. But what are the other elements?

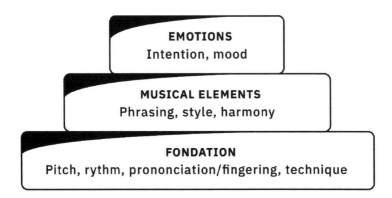

I have divided these elements into three groups, one for each level of the pyramid. I have separated and classified the elements to better address them, although I am very conscious they are linked or woven together when we make music.

The foundation or base:

To build our pyramid we need a solid foundation. We need to learn the pitches and the rhythms (that step is often a long, strenuous process). Depending on your instrument you need to figure out fingering, decide on bow strokes, maybe make a reed or learn the correct pronunciation; and finally there is the pure, technical aspect.

For me technique is not only about the accuracy and efficiency of playing the right notes, it is the process by which you free sounds in order to serve your musical and emotion intentions. The sound you will produce is your signature, you own unique expression. Three pianists playing the same instrument will draw a different quality of sounds. Each singer has a recognizable and unique voice. That is also a big part of building a good technique.

The musical elements:

For me, the number one musical element is the phrasing. The organisation, the grouping, the relationship between the notes we produce. Some call it the direction of the phrase that comes from the use of crescendo and decrescendo, accents, articulations, rubato etc. Others call it the gesture of the phrase. Use whichever terms inspire you to keep the musical discourse alive.

I include in the musical elements, the difference of style. A French baroque piece like Rameau or Lully will not require the same rubato, sound production, or occupy the same emotional space as a French Impressionist work by Debussy or Ravel.

The harmonic component is also an important aspect of the musical elements. Each new chord creates a different color, impact and emotion. The instrumentalists and singers need to react accordingly if the harmonic discourse is suddenly interrupted by an unexpected chord, or if the end of the phrase is suspended instead of resolved.

The emotional content or the message:

Finally, I place at the top of the pyramid the emotional component—the soul of the music, the intention behind each phrase. The life of the music is often associated with the rhythm, and for me the meaning of that life, the purpose is linked with the emotions carried through the sounds we make.

I usually ask musician for eight to ten adjectives to describe what the mood of a piece is. And I specify to also include the shadow of the main emotion. For example, if the beginning of the piece is kind of happy, sunny, in love, light, humorous, mischievous, the shadow, or the ten percent of hidden emotion could be a sense of urgency, maybe doubts, fear of losing, etc.

When I present this structure in a conference or a workshop, I usually ask at the end, which level do you think is the most important one?

That is a tricky question. Some people say it is the foundation. Then I ask them "If you go to a concert and the elements of the base are excellent but the musical elements and the emotional connexion are not present, what do you think of that performance?"

They usually say "it's boring, or I'll leave at intermission." It is a little like a student recital. It is a necessary step in the process of mastering your ability, even if it is still an incomplete one.

If they say it is the top of the pyramid, then I will suggest that if the emotional connection is very intense with a great sound for example, but many details like the rhythm, the notes, the pronunciation (if it is a singer) or the musical elements are barely there, it probably sounds more like a talented amateur than an accomplished professional.

Imagine that each of these elements represent a different ball. When you make music, you will probably connect with the emotion, make the first sound, readjust that sound production for the second one, then organized those two sounds, with a direction to either crescendo or decrescendo. It is as if you are juggling with each of those balls, alternating, returning to one, jumping to another one depending of the need in the moment.

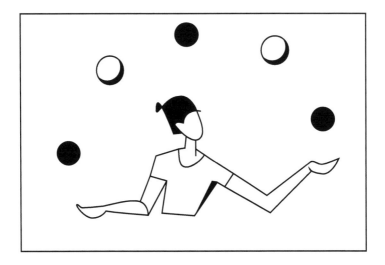

If I were to ask you what is your job as a musician? A good analogy would be to juggle with all those musical elements. What would be your ball number one? Number two? And then you alternate with which one? From a purely Cartesian point of view, it could be very useful to explore how you would organize and play with all of those elements.

If you are preparing for an orchestra audition, with many very short excerpts, I would suggest that you choose two or three words specifically designed to address your needs for each very short passage. They could be mood adjectives, physical cues to keep you grounded or just a reminder of the kind of energy you need to channel in order to play each excerpt.

Now that your outer game is clearer, it is time to tie it with your inner game. You will use your own personal negative tendencies and find two or three solutions or ways to react when they present themselves.

4. Implantation of Intention

Inspired and based on the same format of the road or the cliff exercise, you will clarify on the left side of a page your negative tendencies when under stress (your cliff). Then you will transform them into what you want instead, or how you want to react (you can use the elements of your pyramid) on the right side of the same page (your road).

You remember that to feel stress when under pressure is a very normal reaction. It just means that this performance is important to you. You are doing something that you do not do every day and you are out of your comfort zone. Physically and mentally, your body is undergoing a survival response. You are receiving a rush of energy to help you face the challenge. Sometimes this can create unwanted side-effects.

Those disturbing side-effects can take the form of automatic thoughts that occur during your performance (what I call your inner negative dialogue), and they can also appear with some physiological undesired manifestations. You can separate them into two groups: one related to your physical manifestation like hands shaking, tight body parts, sensations, and one related to your mental manifestations like your little negative voice telling you you are too nervous to play well, not to make a mistake, that you will never have a career etc. These are emotions that can overwhelm you.

To help you shed light on your manifestations, you can imagine three different scenarios and write down, after each one, what came up. Let us suppose that you are doing an audition or a competition and the jury absolutely loves you. Does that awaken any thoughts or physical discomfort? Then imagine you perceive that the jury really does not like you and almost seams annoyed. What does that provoke in your head and in your body? And finally, let us pretend that the jury is totally indifferent to what you are doing. Any different manifestations? My goal is to help you find the most complete negative specific reactions you tend to have in a stressful situation in order to prepare your new way of reacting to it.

And as a last step in this elicitation process, can you find a symbol that best summarises all the physical manifestations that you wrote down. It can be as varied as a frozen rabbit in front of a car, a big dark cloud of fog surrounding you, an iceberg, a tornado, a big, heavy rock on top of you, etc. And also find a symbol for all the negative thoughts you're having—maybe something like a prisoner in jail, an old school teacher scolding you or a bully in the school yard.

Once you have made a complete list of the obstacles that can present themselves on the left side of the page, on the right side, for each item in the cliff side, you will find two or three constructive and helpful reactions to those unwanted effects.

When x happens, I do y. And if y doesn't satisfy me, I do z. That is called the implantation of an intention. You are programming a new automatism; you are pairing two things together. Think of it like the Pavlov experiment in classical conditioning: the bell makes the dog salivate even if there is no food, because he had previously associated the sound of the bell with the arrival of his meal.

You may choose your new action either from the pyramid of a musician or from an inspiring personal inner state. You will link this new reaction when a trigger occurs that tends to limit you. You commit to this new resolution because you have made the decision to respond each time with this new action. And you even have another one planed in case the first one does not satisfy you completely.

Here are a few examples of this process:

If, when something happens during the performance, your tendency is to tell yourself you will never have a career, instead, each time this thought comes up, chose to tell yourself something true and inspiring like "I do what I have to do, or I stay connected to the fact that I love music or I bring more love into this, etc."

It is important to choose something that you believe in, and not a positive affirmation that is the exact opposite of the negative thought like thinking "I am wonderful, I'll have a great career" etc. Those thoughts will not be empowering because of the lack of evidence in that instant.

If what comes up is something like "I need to be impeccable, perfect, and make no mistakes." You can choose to create a new direction with a thought like "my job is to have fun, I take care of one phrase at a time, I connect with the direction and the emotion of this phrase and I let go of what just happened (it is too late, I move on)."

In the end, you also transform the two limiting symbolizations into a symbol that corresponds to all the new creation of intention. If you had, for example, a tornado haunting you in the cliff column, maybe you have the image of a Buddha, or a big oak tree, very solid even when there is a lot of wind.

Here is an example

CLIFF Interferences/negative tendencies	ROAD Action/Implantation of Intention
In your head	**In your head**
(inner dialogue/emotions/mental manifestation)	
Ex: I'll never have a career	I do what I have to do/I love to sing/make music
I'm shy/I feel shy	I go for it/ no regret/release each sound
I'm afraid to make a mistake	One phrase at a time/just sing/what's the mood/I play from my center
I need to be correct	I'm here to have fun/make something nice/I love to make something up
Symbol A demon is haunting me	**Symbol** A Sun or Superman flying
In your body	**In your body**
(sensations/physical manifestation)	
Breathing too high	Contract my belly and exhale/ flexible like a balloon
I'm paralysed/I feel frozen	go for it/contract-relax/I love this more than I feel stuck, I can do this,
I feel small	tall/open up/ breath/I'm here to do my job, have the best time I ever had
Symbol A deer in head lights	**Symbol** an eagle/an oak tree

In summary:

CLIFF Interferences/negative tendencies	ROAD Action/Implantation of Intention
In your head	**In your head**
(inner dialogue/emotions/mental manifestation)	
Symbol	**Symbol**
In your body	**In your body**
(sensations/physical manifestation)	
Symbol	**Symbol**

You can also test your implantation of intention in your run-through, especially the physical manifestations. For example, if you tend to breath too high, you can run, jump, go up and down some stairs for two minutes (to manifest the same inner state) and then, without resting, go through your pieces with your new intentions like: I choose to put my focus on the quality of the sound, or I make each sound full of the emotion I decided for that passage or I play or release each sound (instead of looking at the cliff). The solution is to find something inspiring and fun instead of looking at the cliff.

C – Short-Term goal/your goal for today's performance:

Now that you have clarified your deep motivation (long term goals), and that you have many specific actions planed for your performance (goals of action), all you need now is a simple, clear direction for this specific performance. If you have an audition every day this week, you need to adjust your short-term goal for each day. I am talking about a general direction that will represent the big dome that overlooks your goals of action.

Every performance has a different stake. Sometimes the challenge is charged emotionally for personal reasons, like someone on the jury is making you nervous, or the issue of this audition is important for your career or perhaps this audition is not very charged and it is dangerous that you will not be as focused as you need in order to give your best. What can you tell yourself or what decision do you need to make in order to get as much peace of mind as possible?

Here are a few questions to help you clear the air surrounding your upcoming performance:

5. Your short-term goal

What is the challenge today? What are you afraid of?
What are your expectations for this particular performance?
What do you want to be able to say when you walk out on stage?
Write down everything that comes up, do not censure yourself.

For each of those issues, figure out what would be the best way to counter-act that difficulty.

Here are few examples that came up when helping musicians prepare for a competition:

- No matter what happens, go for it, keep going, no judgements
- One breath at a time, one musical phrase at a time
- It is between me and my instrument, me and the music
- This is my time, no regrets

Maybe for each piece, you have a different issue. For example, if you are afraid to push in the first piece you may choose to say "easy tiger, smooth sailing, just let the music go." If in the second one, your tendency is to hold back, say "go for it, out with it, easy and solid like a rock."

Maybe some of your recurrent issues were already addressed when you did the Implantation of Intention. You can use them here.

One soprano I worked with was preparing for the Tchaïkovsky Competition. When I asked her what her goal was and what she wanted to be able to say after her performance, she said "I want to be calm and sing like when I'm alone."

It did not seem realistic for me considering the high-pressure event she was going to and her usual inner state in previous competitions. We explored the upcoming situation and she realized that wanting to perform as if she were in her living room was not the best strategy. She instead chose to go with "I'm focussed, driven, I use all my energy to give my best." That gave her the general direction she needed.

In summary:

What is the challenge today?

What are you afraid of?

What are your expectations for this particular performance?

What do you want to be able to say when you walk out on stage?

Use all this information to create a simple and empowering statement.

6. Suggestions for the Final Formulation

Writing down what you want to accomplish can have a big impact, yet apparently only 3% of people write down their goals. Many people take more time to write out their grocery list than to put down on paper what is most important in their lives. According to some studies, writing down a goal and putting it in a place where you can see it increases your chances of reaching it by 39%. Remember the old saying "out of sight, out of mind." Keep your goal visible so that it stays alive with you.

As much as possible, try using a formulation that is short. A good way to empower yourself is to start your goal with *I* and use a verb in the present tense (not conditional as in "I would like to…"). It could be as simple as I walk on stage full of energy, or I am here to have fun. If you prefer the formulation with "I want", that can work too, as in I want to walk on stage full of energy or I want to have fun. Play with both and choose the one that feels stronger for you.

Find a symbolic representation, like an image, a person, an animal, an object, or a symbol, that connects you to your goal, and put it with your written objective. Your unconscious will have much more substance to work with and be able to go much deeper if you speak to it in its language—imagination.

If you can imagine it, you can do it.
Walt Disney

You can also feed your inner drive to reach your goal by actively and regularly involving your imagination by making a collage of all the different aspects of your goal. It is a fun exercise that I do at least once a year to give myself a clear direction, whether it is for a specific challenge or just for life in general.

In summary:
Write your goal, starting with *I* + the verb in the present tense, put it up where you can see it. Finally, add a symbolic representation of your goal; you can also make a collage with as many images as you wish.

7. Bonus material
When I work on the formulation of a goal, I always keep in mind three criteria:

A - Positivity:
That's the one I used to build the exercise, i.e. the road versus the cliff. Your brain cannot make a representation of a negative. Whenever you come up with something you do not want any more, write it down first. It is precious information, then take a moment to figure out what the positive version would be.

B - Initiated and maintained only by you:
In his book *The Mental Game Plan*, sports psychologist Stephen Bull makes an important distinction between an outcome goal and a process goal.

If your goal is to win the race, the competition, or the audition (the outcome), your long-term preparation is strongly motivated by this goal, but the closer you get to performance day, the more you will have to bring your focus on the process, more specifically, on the actions to be accomplished during the performance (like we did with the goals of action).

The reason is that you have no control over the outcome of the competition, but you do have control over what you will do during your performance. This is why you want to formulate your goal in such a way that you are the only one in charge or responsible to initiate and maintain it.

Instead of thinking of winning the competition in the future, think about how you want to be during the performance (stay in the now). How do you want to behave? How do you want to react? To Feel? What do you want to do?

Many singers for example, want the public to love them. It is emotionally legitimate—we all want people to like what we do—but it is not really helpful as a goal because it is not up to you whether they love you or not. You have no power over what the public will think.

You can either explore the question of what do I need to do or to be to have the most chances of winning the audience's love. That would bring you back in the driver's seat because it will come from yourself. Or you can ask yourself what will reaching that goal bring you. If you answer that you would feel connected to them, that is excellent, now, how can you achieve a better connection with them? Maybe you would answer by really loving what I do, or stay really connected with yourself and the mood of the music, or just stay open.

If you answered the question "what will reaching that goal bring me" with: I would feel loved, then I would suggest that you bring that feeling of being loved with you on stage. You can use a memory, not one relating to performing but one of a moment you felt really loved in your personal life, to spark your energy.

If we look at goals from a social cognitive psychology point of view, instead of using outcome and process goals, they propose performance goals versus mastery goals. Performance goals focus on comparing ourselves with others, whether your inner motivation is to demonstrate that you have better capacities than others, or if you are driven by a desire to avoid failure relative to others. When you want to win the audition or the competition, your focus is on a performance goal.

The mastery goal's aim is to learn and eventually mastering a difficult task. You want to improve your ability and master new skills. It brings you back in the present moment. That is why performance goals tend to generate a lot of stress whereas mastery goals lead you toward playfulness, curiosity and the pleasure to discover what will make you grow.

Is your goal a mastery goal, fully charged with the possibility of growth and are you 100% responsible for its outcome?

One of my friends is a very successful actor. But he was not always comfortable in auditions. I remember several years ago when Carl told me he had started to shift his attitude during his auditions. He realized that his job was not to get the part or win the audition. Since he had no control of the end result, his job was to share his craft and passion—to be as true as possible to the text, the character and bring as much enthusiasm in the present moment during his audition. That shift helped him bring his creativity and talent into what he was doing. As a musician, I could really relate to those words and it helped me reconnect to my deeper motivation and sense of pleasure each time I walked into an audition.

Goal vs. Expectation: What is your mindset?

Big potential, like genius, creativity and inspiration, is not something you HAVE, it is something you tap into.

Shawn Achor [11]

Figuring out your goal gives you a direction. It allows you to make sure you are on a path that is coherent and aligns with your values, with what is important for you. Now, if I want to be thorough, I have to say that it is only part of the equation. Clarifying what you want is extremely important, but to shed light on your expectations is also crucial because it will help you stay focused on the things that you have power over.

Some people think that having high expectations is the best strategy to grow. Others will choose to focus their attention on lowering their expectations, to make them more realistic and build more self-confidence. They are actually both right, or both excellent strategies as long as your expectations come from a growth mindset.

Stanford professor Carol Dweck discovered that some people see intelligence or abilities (in your case: musical talent) as fixed — it is called the "fixed mindset". Those people believe that their intelligence or talent is innate and unchangeable—fixed in the sense of fixed at birth.

Other people, meanwhile, see their abilities as qualities that can be developed — a growth mindset. They believe that their intelligence or talent is a starting point for a much longer learning process (like the 10 000 hours to mastery in the introduction).

We need to realize that we are not chained to our current capabilities. Neuroscience shows that the brain is very malleable, and we can change and improve our own ability to think and to perform. Every time we push ourselves out of our comfort zone to learn something new and difficult, the neurons in our brain can form new, stronger connections (new neuro pathways), and over time, we get smarter,

Brain scans show that for people with a fixed mindset, the brain becomes most active when receiving information about how the person performed, such as a grade or a score. But for people with a growth mindset the brain becomes most active when

11 Shawn Achor, *Big Potential,* P.43

receiving information about what they could do better next time. In other words, people with a fixed mindset worry the most about how they are judged, while those with the growth mindset focus the most on learning. And research also shows that we have the power to change our mindsets.

Sometimes we win, sometimes we ~~lose~~ learn something.

John Maxwell

Adding "yet" or "not yet"

To develop a growth mindset is in direct link with a mastery goal. To explore the elements that will help you improve and grow is the opposite of praising innate talent or criticizing the end results. If you nurture and promote the process, the efforts and perseverance, you will change the popular saying "practice makes perfect" into "practice makes progress". Because progress makes you proud, it brings happiness.

Our tendency to buy into the perfectionist view of life negates our human nature and keeps us locked into a performance goal aiming only for the end result. And that result needs to be first place. It is an all-or-nothing way of thinking. That is, a fixed mindset. By opening up to a wider view and aiming for excellence instead of perfection, you already make a step towards growth.

To help you cultivate that growth mindset, listen carefully to your inner dialogue, and when you hear phrases like: "I can't do it", simply add: "I can't do it *yet*". Just like we did in the art of reframing. The kids in Dweck's studies where able to develop more confidence because of the training in growth mindset. The teachers praised the process they engaged in, their efforts, their focus and their perseverance,—and by developing this habit of adding yet or not yet. Dweck's message to the parents was that if you want to give your children a gift, teach them to love challenges. Help them be intrigued by mistakes. When they learn to enjoy the effort they will keep on learning and tap into their potential.

> **My fear of making a mistake seems to be based on the hidden assumption that I am potentially perfect and that if I can just be very careful, I will not fall from heaven. But a mistake is a declaration of the way I am, a jolt to the way I intend, a reminder that I am not dealing with facts. When I have listened to my mistakes, I have grown."**
>
> *Hugh Prather*

C-Sensory based indicators:

Studies in psychology have demonstrated that people who reach their goals take time to build a clear mental representation of what they want. It is interesting to notice that how we get there is not the most important factor, but to imagine in detail how it is going to be when we reach it is the actual game-changer. Therefore, your goal will have more impact if it is defined and evaluated according to sensory-based evidence.

How will you know that you have arrived at your goal? This might seem obvious at first, but the idea is to find as many details as possible to guide your unconscious. You will favour sensory-based indicators of success. This will act as a GPS address for your unconscious mind. The exact address implies "being as specific as possible."

You can provide sensory-based indicators by answering questions like:

What will I see? (what will others see?)
What will I hear? (what will others hear?)
What will I feel physically
What emotions will I experience?
What will I say to myself? (what will others say?)

Use your imagination to build an inspiring and motivating representation of what you are seeking to achieve. In addition to mapping the road to follow during your performance, having clear indicators that show when each action is successful will allow you to quickly recognize whether or not you are headed in the right direction. This empowering feeling will also help you build up your self-confidence.

For example, if your goal is to play with sounds and tell a story, how will you know that you have reach that goal? If you say: "I will feel good," that is too imprecise and difficult to verify. Take the time to explore a little: "How exactly is that going to happen? How will I know that I am feeling good?" It might be because of something like: "my shoulders are low and relaxed, my breath is steady and full, I feel like I am expanding and ready to fly, I look far and my sense of space is very wide and open, I am starting to smile, I feel naughty, like a child about to pull a prank," etc.

If you like to use visualisation in your mental preparation, I would suggest that you include as much sensory input as you can to make it as real as possible. You can also add a few scenarios that include if something unexpected happens, how will you react? (The same idea behind the implantation of intention exercise.) By preparing a different storyline in advance, you build the skill to adjust easily and smoothly so when something does happen, even if you did not prepare that one, you are ready to react.

In summary:
(Bonus materiel)
Is your goal formulated positively?
Is it a mastery goal (instead of performance goal), a process goal (instead of an outcome goal)?
Do you believe that you can grow (growth mindset instead of fixed mindset)?
What are your sensory-based indicators?
What will I see? (what will others see?)
What will I hear? (what will others hear?)
What will I feel physically?
What emotions will I experience?
What will I say to myself? (what will others say?)

The Child in the Staircase
When a child starts to walk and comes across a little wall, he examines it until he finds a way to get over it. He then arrives at a plateau and finds himself in front of another wall. Fascinated, he continues his ascent, arriving at another plateau and—oh joy!—another wall.

He does not say to himself "This is hard! When will life stop putting obstacles in my way?" On the contrary, he loves to discover, to go forward, to explore and live new experiences. His thirst for discovery is unquenchable.

An adult who watches this scene knows that the child is climbing stairs; the child, however, does not know what stairs are.

When performing, the possibilities for growth and testing your limits are infinite. The stairs are a never-ending climb. The child's delight comes not from reaching the top but from the joy of moving towards new conquests.

You were this child. You are still this child. It is this strength, this determination, and this pleasure derived from discovering and exploring that I want to awaken in you, allowing you to climb all the mountains of your most cherished dreams.

CHAPTER 4
CALMING YOUR INNER DIALOGUE
(CENTERING AND FOCUSING YOUR THOUGHTS)

List of tools in this chapter:

Concentration tools
1. Counting inhale/exhale
2. Add a mantra
3. Imagination, balloon + happy memory
4. Sensory Spiral
5. Coherence of the heart

Centering tools
6. Dilts centering
7. Green centering

Master key:
8. Mindfulness

A few years ago, there was a television program showing the mental preparation of the acrobatic skier, Alexandre Bilodeau. During one segment, we saw Alexandre working with a specialist in neurofeedback. (Neurofeedback is a training method based on electrical brain activity, in which self-regulation training allows a better communication with the central nervous system.) He was hooked up to a computer, with sensors attached to his ears and on his body that measured his pulse, breathing, and muscle tension, as well as the temperature and moistness of his hands. By performing different mental and breathing exercises, he was supposed to learn to simultaneously control his body and mind. In other words, to build a switch that turns on his inner calm on demand, both mentally and physically.

During one of the more advanced tests, we could see on a screen a mouse that would start walking only when Alexandre's brain gave off certain waves, corresponding to a state of inner calm and concentration. In this way, Alexandre was learning how to put his mind in a deep state of concentration that made the mouse move forward, on command.

After seeing the mouse take a few steps forward, he said to himself, surprised, "Cool! I can do this!" and immediately the mouse moved backwards.

First lesson: It is possible to create at will this calm and to focus inner state. Second lesson: You cannot be concentrated and comment to yourself at the same time. You can only be in one mental state at a time.

As I mentioned in Chapter One, Flow works as a cycle. And the second step of that cycle is the release (or relaxation)—the detachment necessary to go through the doorway of that amazing inner state. That process can be measured and understood thanks to the electrical activity in your brain. The progress of science in that department will help you develop the ability to slow down, on demand, your mental activity.

I will show you some simple concentration exercises, some centering practices, and an introduction to mindfulness meditation to help you achieve a calmer inner state at will. Notice that I did not say stop your inner dialogue or shut it off, but to calm your inner dialogue. That nuance will be important to keep in mind as you go through the following exercises. It is the key ability to enter the Flow, and you will be able to develop it, like any other skill, with a good plan and some repetitions.

When you are stressed out, your brain goes into hyper-activity which corresponds to the high range of your Beta waves. That state consumes too much energy to allow you to perform at your best. Here is an overview of the five major brain-waves types (as measured by an EGG, electroencephalogram), each corresponding to a different state of consciousness.

Beta: between 14 Hz and 30 Hz, signifies learning and concentration at the low end, fear and stress at the high.
Alpha: Between 8Hz and 13.9 Hz, the brain's basic resting state. People in alpha are relaxed, calm, lucid, but not really thinking.
Theta: between 4Hz and 7.9 Hz, which correlates to REM sleep, meditation, insight and the processing of novel incoming stimuli.
Delta: the slowest brain wave. Between 1Hz and 3.9 Hz. When someone is in a deep, dreamless sleep.[12]

12 Steven Kotler, _The Rise of Superman_, P.33

BRAINWAVES

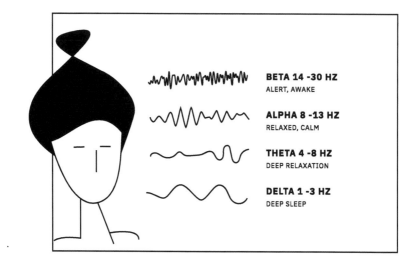

Our brain uses two distinct systems to process information. The explicit and the implicit system. The explicit system is tied to our conscious awareness. It is very logical, organized and can be verbally expressed. It shows on an EGG as your Beta waves. If I use an analogy, it is like when in a factory, all the workers are doing the same thing at the same time.

The implicit system switches on when the analytical and logical system is swapped out for a more instinctive, gut feeling process. In the factory analogy, it corresponds to a big assembly line where the workers do a different action working in a collaborative process to achieve a collective goal. That is your low Alpha/high Theta wave.

There are two advantages for the brain to use the implicit system. The first is speed. Automatization permits much quicker decision-making. It is only when the slow system of your conscious brain is pushed to the back of the queue that your implicit system can do its best work. The second advantage is efficiency. Our brain consumes 20% of our energy and our explicit system is not energy efficient. It uses a lot of power to make those conscious connections.

Since low Alfa/high Theta is the dominant brain wave produced by our implicit system, it is considered the frequency of high performance and Flow state. More recent research has added a little clarification to this conclusion. Studies on athletes have shown that they actually moved through this entire cycle of brain waves fluidly. Instead of being exclusively in one state, they transition between states smoothly and with control. That means that during a performance, when you are in the Flow, you are dominantly using low Alfa/high Theta brain waves while sometimes moving in and out, depending of the different needs of the moment.

It might be surprizing to you that instead of becoming hyperactive during a performance requiring high cognitive functions, your prefrontal cortex (explicit system) is temporarily deactivated.

It's an efficiency exchange. ---The technical term for this exchange is transient hypo frontality, with hypo (meaning slow) being the opposite of hyper (i.e. fast)----when people lose themselves in a task (be it playing cards or having sex or climbing a mountain) a part of the brain called the superior frontal gyrus starts to deactivate. The superior frontal gyrus helps produce our sense of self. That introspective feeling of self-awareness.[13]

The result is liberation. We act without hesitation. Creativity becomes more free-flowing, risk taking becomes less frightening. Your sense of self disappears, and time perception is altered. You are in the Flow.

Without a calm, relaxed frame of mind, the brain is incapable of switching from beta-dominant localized networks to alpha-driven widespread webs.[14]

Now that you know what is happening inside your head, the question is: How can you develop this fluidity of brain activity?

Concentration tools:

1. Counting inhale/exhale

The easiest way I have found to slow down your automatic thought patterns and stay in the present moment is this simple focusing exercise. It is an excellent first step if you have never done anything like this before because it can be done anywhere and at any time.

First, get in touch with your body. I usually propose to start sitting up, with your back strait. Close your eyes and for the next three to five minutes, keep your body as calm as possible, ideally immobile. Hold your breath for four or five seconds and then exhale. You can do that a couple of times. It will send the signal to your brain that you are entering a different state and act as a kind of reset for your body and mind.

13 Steven Kotler, *The Rise of Superman*, P.49
14 Steven Kotler, *The Rise of Superman*, P.40

If you prefer, you can also start with contracting some parts of your body, holding it for a few seconds, then exhaling and relaxing. It is the same idea of the Contract/Relax exercise in the last-minute tools chapter. You can also do the contract/relax twice for each body part and then let your breathing return to its natural rhythm.

The key of this concentration exercise is to use a tool to keep your mind focus on your breathing. Counting will act as a gentle guiding assistant. You will count, slowly on the inhale. Let us imagine that it takes you three seconds to breathe in, and as you exhale, gently elongate or extend the time it takes compared to the inhale, let us say maybe four or five seconds. Be gentle, without forcing anything.

You can do five or six cycles of inhale/exhale and then you stop counting. You can just observe your breathing going in and out...Your breath cycle will become calmer and lighter—maybe more and more gently, as if it is almost in slow motion... Or as if it is happening all by itself. Instead of pulling the air in, imagine that it is just filling you up.

You can use that observation moment to relax your tongue. Just notice what is happening. If your thoughts start to make too much noise in your head, or become too active, do another cycle of counting and gently lengthen your exhale.

If you prefer, you can count the same numbers back and forth but counting slower on the exhale.

In summary:

(Inhale) 1 - - - 2 - - - 3 - - - - (Exhale) 1 - - - - - - - 2 - - - - - - 3 - - - - - - 4 - - - -
Or
(Inhale) 1 - - - 2 - - - 3 - - - 4 - - - - (Exhale) 4 - - - - - - - 3 - - - - - - 2 - - - - - 1 - - - - - - 0 - - - - etc.

Some days it is easier and some days it takes more effort. Imagine that your conscious brain, the part of your brain that thinks, is a little puppy that has never been trained and has never learned to walk with a leash. The counting becomes the leash for your brain. Remember that the goal is not to stop your thinking process completely, but to realize that you and the part of you that thinks, can be separated. You have thoughts—but you are not your thoughts.

Here are a few suggestions to help you become comfortable with this practice:
- You can do this sitting on a chair or a cushion. The point of the practice is to be reasonably comfortable and alert without falling asleep, so it is natural to experience some light

physical discomfort. And if you only have three or four minutes, you may also explore this standing up. I do it sometimes while waiting for the bus or the subway.

- When you are sitting upright, imagine that you have a string attached to the top of your head that is pulling you slightly toward the sky. When your head is in line with your spine your energy runs differently through your body. Once in a while, during the exercise, you can check that you are still aligned with your vertical axis by pulling your chin back a quarter of an inch.
- You can keep your eyes open if it is more comfortable for you. You can look at an object like a candle, an image, a picture, a rock, or a plant that you have placed at about four or five feet in front of you while keeping a relaxed gaze.
- You may want to use a timer and decide before you start how long this session will last. That way you can stay focussed until the end without worrying about missing an appointment. That sense of security will allow your brain to come back to the process, each time it wanders, instead of giving in to the urge of checking the time or ending the practice.
- Choose a time that is convenient for you. I suggest to link the practice with an activity that you have to do each day, for example, before you eat, before you brush your teeth, or before you start practicing.
- Imagine that your brain is like a snow globe. Inside the globe there is a beautiful castle. That castle is you, your true self. It is the part of you that is observing. The snow represents your thoughts, your beliefs, your emotions and your physical sensations. Most of the time, there is a snow storm with glitter flying around your brain. When you stop for a moment to do a concentration exercise or to meditate, your mind will settle down, or at least become quieter. If you try too hard to clear your mind, you may end up creating more tension and shaking your globe up. Instead of imposing stillness on your mind, just observe what is happening. Take a little distance and just be present as you watch the snow gently moving. Remember, it is not about stopping your thoughts, it is about being present and observing the inner activity.

During my workshops, I suggest to the participants to take a two-week challenge. You do one version of the concentration exercises proposed in this chapter, twice a day, five minutes each time, for two weeks, and then decide if the benefits outdo the cost. I encourage you to be flexible in your exploration. Approach each of these practices with curiosity and an open mind and do not hesitate to adapt these suggestions to make the experience more fruitful for you.

To give you an alternate way of using numbers with your breathing, you can chose to count the breathing cycle. During the inhalation, you say slowly in your mind: 1...1....1... and during the exhale 1.....1.....1....

When you noticed that your mind has wandered, just repeat the number you were doing. You can see the number in your mind as you say it or you can keep the count on your fingers. You can go up to five breaths in and out, and when it is easy for you, go to ten. If your thoughts are too agitated or disturbing, bring your attention to the movement of the air inside your belly.

In summary:

(Inhale) 1 - - - 1 - - - 1 - - - (Exhale) 1 - - - 1 - - - - - 1 - - - - - - 1 -
(Inhale) 2 - - 2 - - 2 - - 2 - - - - (Exhale) 2 - - - - - - 2 - - - - - - 2 - - - - - 2 - - - -
Go up to 5 or 10

2. Add a mantra

When your thoughts are agitated, your mind will want to resist concentration exercises. To ease this process, you may need a different stabilizing tool to calm those thoughts.

In the first exercise, I suggested the use of numbers. Another useful tool is a mantra. The Sanskrit (the language in which the Hindu religious texts were written) word "mantra" comes from *man*, meaning "thought", or "of the brain", and *tra*, "instrument" or "tool." Loosely translated and put together gives "a tool for thought," or "a tool for improving the mind."

Your mantra can use one or two key words that you repeat over and over. For example, on each exhale, you can say within yourself, "calm" or "I am safe". Pick the word that has the most meaning for you, that will help your beta brain waves shift into alpha or even theta waves.

Breathe in, and just before breathing out, think "very calm." Or you can say to yourself, when breathing in, "deeply," and when breathing out "relax." You can choose your own words and the moment to use them. You can breathe in and, while holding your breath, say to yourself, "totally," then, when breathing out, "centred."

Those who are more visual can use an image to illustrate their keyword. For example, imagine a beautiful lake or a seaside landscape that brings you greater inner calm at the same time you say your key words. You may imagine the words appearing in beautiful letters.

In summary:

Breathe in while saying "I am".
Breathe out saying "safe".

Or:

Breathe in saying "deeply"
Breathe out saying "relax"

One focusing exercise I learned from a mindfulness teacher is to bring together the awareness of the breath and the use of words.

(On the inhale) I inhale deeply
(On the exhale) I exhale slowing down
(On the inhale) Deeply
(On the exhale) Slowing down
(On the inhale) Inhale
(On the exhale) Exhale

Then you start the whole sequence again and you repeat it for several minutes. You can choose words that are meaningful to you like:

(On the inhale) I inhale strength
(On the exhale) I exhale joy
(On the inhale) strength
(On the exhale) joy
(On the inhale) Inhale
(On the exhale) Exhale

Make it fun and meaningful for you.
Also, a visual element, such as a candle, can serve as a support. Perhaps in the past you have stared at the flames of a fire and noticed they are always the same yet never identical. It is very hypnotic, and ideal for modifying your mental activity.

Look at the flame of a candle and, after a few minutes, when your thoughts have calmed, close your eyes and keep seeing that flame. You may bring your attention back to your breathing as often as you want all throughout this process. In this way, you can alternate between "being conscious of your breathing," and "watching the flame in front of you or in your head."

This list is far from exhaustive, and these are only a few suggestions of possible supports among many. The goal is to alternate between some form of guiding tools and the observation of breathing, and eventually putting aside the support and simply "surfing the wave" of your breathing and staying present.

I must admit that I have been doing some version of these concentration exercises every day for the past thirty years. It is not because you have run a marathon once that you never have to work out ever again. Your mind, just like your body, does not work that way. The more in shape you are, the easier it is to work out and stay in shape. And the depth of the experience also becomes more thrilling.

3. Use your imagination

Before you start, chose a memory of a very happy moment. Something that brings a smile to your face. It can be a hug of someone you deeply love, it could be a memory of holding a baby in your arms, or a magical moment in nature during your last vacation.

On the inhale, imagine that you have a balloon in your chest that you are filling up. Take time to feel it in the front, the side and the back of your body. And on the exhale, bring up the images of the memory you chose and imagine that the memory explodes all around you, showering you with a sparkle of joy and wellbeing associated with that moment. On the next inhale you let your balloon fill up with air, maybe it is more in your belly this time, and on the side of your back, and on the exhale, you revisit your memory that illuminates your whole body.

You do a few cycles of inflating the balloon and contacting the happy memory and then you just observe your breath for a few cycles. You may alternate with counting for a few cycles, then using a mantra, then back to the balloon.

Remember, I suggest you experiment gradually, once or twice a day for five minutes to start. Little by little, you can work your way up to ten, then twenty minutes if you want. At the beginning, some people will need five minutes to get the process going, then they will ride the wave of inner calm for five more minutes. Many have felt a huge difference in their inner state after only two weeks of five minutes a day. Explore at your own pace.

In summary:

On the inhale, imagine that you are a balloon and you are filling up with air.

On the exhale, bring up the images of the memory and let the happy sensations and well-being associated with it explode all around you.

Do a few cycles of inhale/exhale then just observe your breathing.

You can do another round of this imagination tool, or alternate with counting or a mantra, as you prefer.

4. The Sensory Spiral

The next exercise is inspired by a technique often used in self-hypnosis. To help you focus your attention, it uses three senses: what you see, what you hear, and what you feel. To start, keep your eyes open in order to create a smooth transition between your "normal state of consciousness" and the state of concentration you are aiming for.

Choose a specific point to look at and blink as little as possible. Without blinking, this intense focus will gradually make your eyes tired. Eventually you will close them with relief.

While fixing that point, you will name three things you see on the periphery, letting five seconds go by between each phrase, or if you prefer, letting a cycle of breath—inhale/exhale—go by between each thing named.

For example:

I notice the colour of the wall around the point.

(During the five-second pause, let yourself be immersed in this colour of the wall.)

I notice the lighting in the room.

(Take five second pause, while you become conscious of the lighting.)

And I notice the painting that is to the left of the fixed point.

(Take another five second pause while you let yourself be absorbed by the sight of the painting).

Still keeping your eyes open and fixed on the point, you will name three things that you hear, still taking five seconds in-between each thing.

For example:

I hear the rain outside.
(During the pause, you are curious about the effect this sound has on you, and perhaps you are having trouble keeping your eyes open, but you resist).
I hear the ticking of the clock...
(Take a five second pause to let yourself be rocked by the ticking).
I hear the sound of my own breath...
(Take a five second pause during which you pay attention to all the nuances of the sound of your breath).

Still staring at the point and pausing for five seconds in-between, you will name three things that you feel in your body.

For example:

I feel my chest rising, filling with each breath...
(Pause for five seconds).
I feel my hands in contact with my thighs...
(Pause. Perhaps you are having more and more difficulty keeping your eyes open).
I feel a tingling, a slight numbing in my right shoulder...
(Pause for five seconds).

You will now do this a second time, this time naming only two things of which you are conscious (see, hear, feel), still pausing between each thing you name. Once your eyes cannot stay open anymore, you can let them shut, even if you are in the middle of the process. You can continue this spiral, naming the images that come to you instead of what you physically see.

You will end with a final round, only naming one thing you see followed by a pause, one thing you hear plus a pause and one thing you feel. Stay in this state of inner calm, observing the wave of your breath, enjoy it for a few minutes before ending this concentration exercise.

In summary:
(Choose and fix a point)

1st Round
Name three things that you see with your peripheral vision, pausing for five seconds (or the time to inhale and exhale) between each element named.
Name three things that you hear with a pause of five seconds between each.
Name three things that you feel with a pause of five seconds between each.

2nd Round (Still staring at the fixed point)
Name two things that you see with a pause of five seconds between them.
Name two things that you hear with a pause of five seconds between them.
Name two things that you feel with a pause of five seconds between them.

3rd Round (Still staring at the fixed point, or closing your eyes)
Name one thing that you see, then pause for five seconds.
Name one thing that you hear and pause for five seconds.
Name one thing that you feel and pause for five seconds.

Enjoy this state of inner calm for a few minutes.

5. Coherence of the heart

HeartMath, an American institute of neurocardiology, discovered several years ago that the *"communication between the brain and the heart is a dynamic, ongoing, two-way dialogue, with each organ continuously influencing the other's function."* [15]

Researchers have discovered that our emotions have an effect on the heart-rate variability (HRV) – the beat-to-beat changes in heart rate, as well as on the way that the brain processes information. For example, frustration or fear causes an irregular and chaotic heartbeat, which inhibits centres in the brain and alters our capacity to react. On the other hand, other emotions, such as love or gratitude, will do the opposite, creating a more harmonious and regular heartbeat as well as allowing for a greater ability to react.

15   *Internet site: heartmath.org, science of the heart.*

When you engage in specific exercises, similar to the concentration ones you just did, your heartbeat becomes more harmonious. An image similar to an electrocardiogram (ECG) clearly shows waves in hyperactivity (called incoherence), during activities such as a difficult mathematical calculation, or when we judge ourselves harshly. Then, thanks to a specific exercise, the line becomes more regular as the mind slows down, and coherence is established with the heart.

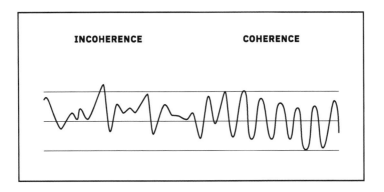

Four Key Inner States

The research revealed that some inner states were particularly effective to generate quickly this coherence. Those four coherence magnets are: gratitude, non-judgment, forgiveness, and care. They are unique because they are able to create a very powerful emotion that facilitates the coherence between the heart and the mind. An excellent way of experiencing them is to revisit the memory of an important event during which you felt a profound connection to one of these states.

This connection creates in you a feeling of letting-go, a sense of well-being and even an openness at the level of the heart. You can choose a memory linked to something important you have accomplished (gratitude), a situation where compassion was particularly present (a state of non-judgment), an act of reconciliation (forgiveness), or remember a moment when you took care of someone you love (care). I suggest you explore these states one by one to find out which one is easier to access and works best for you.

Here is a simple and powerful exercise that uses the same first steps as in the concentration exercise while adding a new support: a memory of one of the four inner states.

Whenever using a memory, it is important to take the time to revisit that memory with as many sensory connections as possible: see the place, the people, the objects, the colours; smell the odours; hear the noises, the sounds, the conversations, what you said to yourself; feel what happened in your body as if you were there again. Relive everything with sincerity and as deeply connected as possible.

First Step: Get in touch with Your Body
It is usually easier to start while sitting, both feet on the ground, hands on your thighs or on the armrests. Keep your body as still as possible during this exercise and avoid parasitic movements. The body's calm will influence the mind and invite it to calm down as well.

Second Step: Observe Your Breath
Become aware of the movement of your breath flowing through your body. Be attentive to the sensations in your body that are linked to your breathing.

Do you feel the path that the air is taking throughout your body? Its entry through your nostrils? Your mouth? Can you feel the air entering you and going down into your lungs? Do you feel your chest rising? Your ribs expanding? Let your breaths grow longer without forcing, just because it is more fun to take your time.

Third Step: Use a Memory and Place Your Hand on Your Heart
Recall the happy memory you have chosen, whether it be a memory of gratitude, compassion, forgiveness, or care, and place your hand on your heart. This memory can be as simple as the love you feel for a special person (care) or an inspiring place in nature that you love (gratitude), like the beach during your last vacation or a memorable sunset. Once the connection with the memory is made, imagine that you are breathing through your heart while you explore the images, the sounds, the smells, the sensations of that moment.

Breathe the emotion in and out through your heart and remain in this state for five to ten minutes. Research done at the HeartMath Institute showed that ten minutes of cardiac coherence had a lasting effect of several hours on many systems of the body.

In summary:
Keeping your body still, bring your awareness to your breathing, (you can do a few minutes of the previous concentration exercises if you wish),
Then place your hand on your heart and contact the memory you have chosen (gratitude, forgiveness, non-judgment, care).
Breath through your hand as you explore that memory with all your senses.

Centering tools:

6. Centering à la Dilts

The word "centering" refers to the concentration of attention or energy on something. I like its original meaning as a temporary frame to support an arch or vault during construction until it is able to stand by itself.

With the help of your imagination, you'll create a temporary frame to focus your concentration and energy for the upcoming performance. To create that frame you will bring your awareness to different centers of energy in your body, each symbolizing a member of your inner team.

That team is made of all your inner strength: the intelligence and power of your body, the love and compassion of your heart, the wisdom of your brain and the connection to others and to a force greater than you. Each team member is also associated with a specific body part. You will visit them one by one, while adding a short phrase, a color and a symbol.

First, bring your awareness to your belly. Below the navel, there is an energy center called tantien or hara or chi according to various culture. It is the center associated with the power and the intelligence of your body. As you breath from that center, invoke the phrase: "I am present or I am centered." If you want a stronger association, you can add a color that would go well with that inner state for you, or, if you prefer, a symbol like an object, an animal, a character from a movie or even a person that inspire you this feeling of being present, centered, in the now.

Keeping that first light on, then bring your attention to your heart area, that special place of love and compassion. Breathing now from that center, invoke the phrase: "I am open to give and open to receive." You can also add a color and/or a symbol to anchor this inner state deeper.

While being aware that you are still centered and present in your lower belly and keeping your light and symbol active in the heart area as well, you can move up to your forehead, just a little above your eyes and right in the middle, where some cultures put what they call the third eye. This is the center representing the strength, vivacity and wisdom of your mind. As you breath from that spot, invoke the phrase: 'I am awake, alert, to the signs that come my way." And you also add a color and/or a symbol if you want.

Keeping all your previously visited centers switched on, you finally bring your attention to the top of our head, at the fontanelle (an anatomical feature on an infant's skull).

You will imagine a thread from that point, going straight up to the sky, linking you to the whole universe. Still breathing from that imaginary spot, you invoke the words: "I am connected to others and to something bigger than me."

You can do this sitting or standing up. Take all the time you need to figure out the images and symbols the first time you go through those steps; then the next time it will probably take you just a minute or so to gather your team.

Originally thought as a centering exercise by Robert Dilts to help coaches gather their energy and focus before meeting a client, he was using the acronym C.O.A.C.H. as a way to easily remember that sequence.

In summary:

C = I am centered, present, here (below the navel)

O = I am open to give and open to receive (in the heart area)

A = I am awake, alert, to the signs that come my way (in the forehead/ third eye)

C = I am connected to others and bigger than me (top of the head/fontanelle)

H = I hold that state, that space

At the end, open your eyes, smile and you are ready to go!

7. Centering à la Green

Here is a different centering exercise, inspired by a process that American psychologist, Don Green uses with musicians. It connects your goals of action or short-term goal with a concentration exercise. It is a simple, two steps process: you go in, prepare and contact some key elements and then out, ready for your challenge.

As a preparatory step, you choose the inner state you want to contact and return to at the end. For example, do you want to feel tall? Open? Go-getter? Energized? Confident? Easy-going? Calm? Focus? You chose a spot on a wall in front of you, not too high and not too low. It will be your anchor point to return to at the end.

The first step is the same as in any concentration exercise: you close your eyes, bring your awareness to the breath, you soften the unnecessary tension in the body and then you add an inner representation of a safe space—a place where you can truly be yourself, a place impervious to judgements and fears where you can feel protected and safe. You are perfect the way you are now, your inner light can shine through. The connection with the breath and the body brings you back in the now and with a word, an image or a symbol, you immerse yourself in the ideal space for you to gather your energy.

It can be anything that make sense for you. A blank page, like a painter who needs a blank canvas to paint, or an umbrella like I suggested in Chapter One, to protect yourself from the interferences. Or maybe it is a big, transparent bubble.

The second step serves to connect with your two or three key words chosen from your action goals or short-term goals (formulated in Chapter Three). It can be one word or a short phrase like "open and easy", "stay tall", "look far", "steady flow of air" etc. Breathe slowly and deeply in your belly as you state each key word or phrase.

Finally, you bring all the energy that was in your lower belly up to your head, your control center and open slowly your eyes. It is easier to retain this centered inner state when you come out of this process with a gentle gaze, almost un-focus as you contact your anchor point on the wall. Gradually you will bring more sharpness and focus into your vision without losing your connection with your center. Bring an inner smile and you are ready to go!

You can do this sitting or standing up, take all the time you need to figure out the images and symbols the first time you go through those steps; then, gradually, you will speed up the whole process until it takes you just a minute or two.

In summary:

Intro:
What is your ideal inner state to return to at the end of this centering exercise?
Chose a precise visual point, stay focussed and open.

1st step:
A - Close your eyes + focus your attention on your breathing
B - Soften any tension in your body, (if needed, contact/relax)
C - Create your own inner centering/safe space with a word, image or symbol

2nd step:
A - Say to yourself your key words from your action goals or short-term goal,
(and breath in your lower belly while going through those key phrases).
B - On the next inhale, bring all that energy up into your head and open your eyes,
(keep a gentle gaze on the same fixed point that you started with).
C - Smile and go play your piece or sing your aria

Test this centering process each time you run through your repertoire. If you have no audience to activate your stress hormones, you can record yourself or artificially create usual physical manifestations of stress such as those mentioned before. If your heart beats faster when you perform, you can do some running or jumping for a couple of minutes, then you take only 30 seconds or one minute to center yourself and play your pieces right away.

Be creative, if your hands are usually cold, use an ice pack; if your body is stiff, do some push-ups or sit ups. As much as possible, re-create your body signals of stress.

Green also proposes to figure out your ideal level of activation to perform at your best. Some people perform better when they are a little excited, on a scale of 0 to 10, let us say around five. Others will perform better when they are at three or maybe even at six or seven. Everybody is different.

To figure it out, take your three best performances, and rate them on a scale from 0 to 10 answering: How excited did you feel while performing at your best?

You can take different events like a good audition, a fun orchestra rehearsal, a satisfying recital or opera performance and figure out your best range of excitement for performing. By finding out what works best for you, you can include that level of excitement as your ideal inner state in your centering exercise.

Master key:

8. Mindfulness

After some concentration exercises to calm your inner dialogue and some centering practices to help you prepare to perform, the master tool to develop your ability to focus and open the door to a whole new dimension is mindfulness meditation.

The term mindfulness means different things to different people. This term is used to describe both a particular way of paying attention in the present moment and the practices that help us develop these skills. It is a way to engage in the present moment, without attachment and without judgement. The exercises are designed to train your brain to have more focus and attention as well as better emotional regulation.

It is not a religion, a new age cult, or a hippie concept. It is now science. It is grounded in more than 30 years of scientific study done in the most prestigious universities around the world.

There are thousands of studies demonstrating that mindfulness practice decreases depression, anxiety, and stress; increases overall feelings of well-being, happiness, focus, attention, and academic achievement.

So first, let us clarify the terminology.

What is the difference between meditation and mindfulness?

The essence of meditation is awareness. A basic definition of meditation is moment by moment awareness. An over simplification of the process would be that you sit, still, eyes closed and just observe. That observation position, whether you pay attention to the breath, the sensations in your body or repeat a mantra, will sharpen your skill of staying present.

Meditation is a practice. It is the scales and arpeggios that will help you develop awareness, and it is that awareness that will free you from the automatisms of your thinking process. Meditation is a journey in self-discovery that only you can take. The rewards or the advantages it will bring into your life are countless. Meditation is the tool, the practice that makes mindfulness possible.

Mindfulness is simply about being aware of where your mind is from one moment to the next, with gentle acceptance.[16]

Mindfulness is the opposite of functioning on autopilot. It is the opposite of day-dreaming.

It is a non-verbal experience, that is very difficult to fully capture with words. I will do my best to simplify it although I encourage you to just dive in and experience it first-hand.

There are many different types of meditation. Whether it is a sitting or lying down meditation, walking meditation or standing meditation, the goal is the same: moment to moment awareness. That sounds very simple, right? Here is the catch:

When you meditate, you step back from your everyday life, you narrow your attention, your brain receives less stimulations and it is easier to stay right here in the now. You are teaching your brain that you are the captain of your ship.

But the nature of the mind is to wander. I usually say: the job of your mind is to think. You will not stop it. It is like your breathing. You cannot stop yourself from breathing any more than you can stop yourself from thinking. In fact, you can suspend your breathing probably longer than your thinking.

16   Germer, Siegel, Fulton, *Mindfulness and Psychotherapy,P.xi*

Your goal is not to have no thoughts or to stop thinking but rather to bring yourself back each time you realize that your mind was wandering away. Each time you come back to the present moment, you strengthen the muscles of your brain that will help you stop the automatisms that keep controlling your thought process. Each time you come back to the now, it is like putting money in the bank, it will be very useful when you face a challenge and want to stay present and in the moment, rather than giving way to your fears.

The moment you realize that your mind is wandering is the key. Instead of a moment of failure, see that moment as a moment of success. You were lost and now you are found. It is a journey of friendship with your mind that generates self-acceptance and self-compassion.

The observation of your thoughts creates a space, a distance, a neutral state that will help you truly realize, at a deep level, that you have those thoughts, but you are not your thoughts. There is a part of you that is aware of your thoughts. You could say that there is an intelligence behind your thinking process. This realization creates a disidentification with your thoughts. You are steeping out of your automatic pilot and you can make new choices.

Misconceptions about Mindfulness

Meditation is often though of as shutting ourselves off or clearing our minds. It creates a struggle inside of us. That idea is not very helpful. To go into a blank state is like becoming unconscious. Meditation is not switching off, it is more about switching on, about waking up. It is about expanding our consciousness, to realize that we are more than our thoughts.

Let us imagine that our mind is like the sky. The clouds represent our thoughts and feelings. Some are white and fluffy, and some are dark and heavy. They are part of the sky, but they are not the whole sky. The sky exists behind those clouds, even when they seem to cover the whole sky. Conscious awareness is learning to work with our brain in a new creative way to capture the whole picture.

It is not about achieving a perfect, wonderful, relaxed state of wellbeing or enlightenment, it is about embracing the reality of our present experience. Sometimes we are totally calm, and we may think "ah, that's what meditation is about". But when our mind is turbulent, that is what this moment of meditation is about also. Each time we return to the breath, we strengthen our awareness. We are being the sky instead of the clouds.

It is not about achieving some special feeling, or some special state, it is about recognizing that whatever feeling you are having, or whatever state you are in, you can embrace it with awareness. Through that awareness, you will find new degree of freedom to navigate through the roller coaster ride of your life. Each time you meditate, you will go through different kind of experiences—they are all legitimate and they are all valuable.

Often people use the expression "let it go" when they want to move towards acceptance. Try instead using "let it be". It captures the experience of accepting whatever is present in a gentler way, like inviting a guest to have a seat.

According to Germer, Siegel and Fulton, in their book *Mindfulness and Psychotherapy* there are three types of mindfulness meditation:

1- *Focused attention (or concentration meditation), can be compare to a laser light beam that illuminates any object toward which it is directed.*[17] In concentration practice, you can choose to focus on subtle objects of attention, such as the sensation of the breath entering and leaving the nostrils, or the sensation of the feet touching the ground when walking. Certain mindfulness-building techniques involving imagery help provide stabilization.

The instructions for this type of meditation are very similar to the ones I gave you to calm your inner dialogue (concentration tools) at the beginning of this chapter. They serve as an anchor to gently bring back you mind to the object of attention when you realized that it went wandering.

2 - *Open monitoring can be compared to a searchlight that illuminates a wider range of objects.*[18] The Pali word for this type of meditation is vipassana, which translates as "seeing clearly". You are invited to be receptive and open to sensations, sounds as well as thoughts, emotions or intentions and notice when your attention is taken away.

When you recognize that your mind has wandered, instead of bringing your attention back to your body or breathing, you note what took you attention away (a thought, an emotion, an image, an intention). Instead of identifying with a thought like "I am afraid I cannot do this". You could for example say to yourself "I am having the thought of I cannot do this", or "I notice that I am having a thought that I cannot do this". It helps you see how the mind creates suffering. You can notice the contents of your mind as they arise and greet them with acceptance.

This is a very powerful practice linked to emotional regulation and will have a profound impact on your performance, and more specifically, on your stress management. I will be proposing an exercise to open monitoring at the end of this section.

---

17   Germer, Siegel, Fulton, *Mindfulness and Psychotherapy, P.16*
18   Germer, Siegel, Fulton, *Mindfulness and Psychotherapy, P.17*

3 - *Loving-kindness and compassion describes the quality of mindful awareness—the attitude or emotion—rather than the direction of awareness.*[19] The instruction here is to bring a quality like tenderness, compassion, care or security. The goal with this kind of meditation technique is to sooth and fortify you in order to be able to bear whatever you might experience.

Sometimes, you are dealing with difficult emotions in your life that hinder your awareness. You can use the slow repetition of some phrases like "may I be safe", "may I be peaceful" to invite kindness and compassion into your present experience. You can imagine breathing in the warmth of those phrases for yourself and exhaling that feeling for the benefit of others.

This practice is not meant to avoid the difficulties in your life but rather to give you the calm and strength necessary to be at peace with those emotions. I will further explore this approach in the next chapter with self-compassion.

Finding the optimal balance between concentration, acceptance and loving-kindness practices is an art in itself. That is also why most meditation practices will alternate, often between these three different styles.

A stress reduction tool:

Mindfulness isn't just about the ability to focus and pay attention, it's also a different way to experience emotions like pain, anger, frustration, anxiety, and fear and not react to them automatically. Mindfulness creates a space between our emotions and our responses. Sometimes we forget that joy and pain come and go like ocean waves. Mindfulness allows us to surf, rather than be swept away by the current.

Mindfulness enables us to be reflective and not reactive. It is not about running away from our emotions or not feeling our emotions. It is allowing us not to be overwhelmed by them. It is not about controlling our thoughts and emotions, but rather not having our thoughts and emotions control us.

Imagine how mindful listening could be useful in all your relationships, or how mindful eating could improve your mental and physical well-being and how mindful breathing on a daily basis could allow you to stay calm and focus during a challenging day.

In a performance situation, the stress you experience comes from your own subjective interpretation of that situation. Meditation enables you to observe and catch the various thoughts that lead you to the conclusions that create stress. This new perspective

19   Germer, Siegel, Fulton, *Mindfulness and Psychotherapy, P.19*

allows you to deconstruct this mental process, and within that space, the power to choose.

You can find many inspiring guided meditations on YouTube, the ones most often used by mindfulness therapists are the body scan and the raisin meditation. You might also prefer to go to an evening group meditation. The energy of a group meditating is really empowering and nourishing. Follow your intuition. The benefits of meditation will enrich your life beyond what you can imagine

I leave you with an example of an open monitoring meditation that you can explore by reading it slowly and taking the pauses between the phrases. Or if you prefer, you can record yourself and play it back when you are ready to meditate.

If you have had the opportunity to experience mindfulness before, I suggest you explore this part with a beginner's mind. Suspend for a moment your preconceptions and bring an openness and willingness to discover and just be present as you try out this exercise.

In summary:
Mindfulness guided meditation

Find a quiet place, where you will not be disturbed for the next five to ten minutes, and sit in a comfortable position, on a cushion or on a chair with your back upright without being rigid. Close your eyes partly or completely.

Put aside the story you are telling yourself right now, take a break from your life and bring your attention to your breathing. (pause)

Take two or three slow breaths, imagining that on the inhale you gather any tension remaining in your body and on the exhale, you release and let go gently of all those tensions. (pause)

Let your breathing returning to its natural rhythm, while you check on the level of tension in different parts of your body. Just notice without trying to change anything. (pause)

For the next few breaths, bring your attention to the path of the air travelling in and out of your body. Without trying to control the breath, just notice the sensations... the air coming into your nose or through your mouth.... the way it goes down into your throat.... Into your lungs... maybe you feel that the air is colder on the way in and warmer on the way out... (pause)

Be aware of the different parts of your body that swell as the air comes in and that deflate as the air goes out.... Do you feel it more in the front? The side? (pause) The back?

The lower part of your chest? (pause)

If your mind wanders, that's normal... As soon as you perceive that you went away, take note of the image or thought or emotion that sent you wandering... something triggered your escape from the present moment.... that's ok, no judgements, no criticisms.... just bring yourself gently back to the sensation of sitting here and the movement of your breath. (pause)

Maybe you realize that there is a theme behind your wandering thoughts. Is it more about planning the future? About the past? About a certain emotion? Maybe there is a need behind these thoughts or maybe it will come to you later. (pause)

Let your thoughts come up without engaging with them. Just notice that you are having a thought or a feeling. Let the images appear and stay present to your breath at the same time. Let the images and the thoughts come and go like clouds being carried away by the wind. (pause)

Each time you realize you were distracted, observe what attracted your attention, and then, bring yourself back...here....to your awareness of sitting here and being present to your breathing. (pause)

Imagine a mountain, majestic...Uncompromised by the passing of the seasons. The essence of the mountain remains untouched. Bring the image of that mountain inside you. (pause) You are that mountain. There is a part of you that remains uncompromised through all the events of your life. Feel the stillness, the stability. (pause)

You can also imagine a beautiful waterfall coming through the middle of the mountain. Big cascades of water pour through the rocks. Since you are the mountain, imagine yourself as the rock behind the waterfall. The cascade of water represents your thoughts, constantly pouring out of the mountain. All you have to do is observe that cascade of thoughts flowing from your brain. (pause)

When you are ready to come back, gently open your eyes and take time to stretch a little.

People are like stained-glass windows. They sparkle and shine when the sun is out, but when the darkness sets in, their true beauty is revealed only if there is a light from within.

Elisabeth Kubler-Ross

CHAPTER 5
FACING YOUR FEAR

List of tools in this chapter:

1. Downward Arrow/Worst Case Scenario
2. The Work
3. Don't go NUTS with Stress
4. Emotional Intelligence
5. Self-Compassion
6. Self -Compassion Post-Performance tool: The Evaluation Grid

Man's immortality is not to live forever; for that wish is born of fear. Each moment free from fear makes a man immortal.

Alexander the Great

Our biggest fear is taking the risk to be alive—the risk to be alive and express what we really are.

Don Miguel Ruiz

The last door to unlock to free yourself and unleash your full potential is the door where your fears are hiding. If I use the analogy of a hero's journey, your quest cannot be completed without facing your inner demons and conquering your deepest fears.

Fear lives in the dark. It is very strong and powerful as long as it stays hidden. If you take fear out of the shadow and shine some light on it, it loses half of its strength. When you are nervous, anxious and stressed out about a performance, do you go into denial? Do you hope for the best and then put your head in the sand? In order to transform your relationship with fear, I will show you many ways to shine as much light as possible on it and ultimately, to put that energy to your service.

As I mentioned before, fear, like stress, is an automatic and involuntary response produced by the perception of a threat. That response is initially a survival mechanism very useful to keep us alive but, as we grow up, we generalize that mechanism and create other automatic responses with objects or situations that are no longer real threats. It is then a learned automatism. The good news is we can change that pairing and create new connections with the objects of our fear.

Steven Hayes's metaphor well summarizes this inner turmoil. Our struggle with anxiety or any difficult internal experiences is like a tug-of-war with a giant monster over a hole. The more the monster pulls, the harder we pull back. The monster is pulling us toward the hole, so we resist and pull as much as we can. Maybe our hands are getting torn up by the rope so pulling becomes harder and more painful. We are so afraid to fall into that hole that we keep pulling and resisting. We invest so much time and energy in surviving this tug-of-war, we think that the solution is to use more force.

Finally, we realize we could just drop the rope. It might seem terrifying because we already put so much effort into pulling on that rope and we think that the monster will win. But in reality, the monster does not win at all, we are not falling into the hole. Our hands stop to hurt, and we can choose another direction—like when our automatic response to stress is activated, our natural instinct is to fight, flight or freeze and we keep pulling on the rope. But we can choose another option. Dropping the ropes frees us to live the life we really want. We just need to change strategy.

Where does your stress come from?

Each time you have a concert, a competition or an audition, it creates a reaction in you. That reaction can be pleasant, unpleasant, or a mix of both. You have the impression that the situation creates the emotions you are experiencing. You think the audition is causing the excitement or the stress that makes your hands shake, your heart beats faster or makes you want to run away.

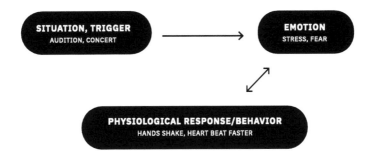

In reality, it is not the situation that creates the emotion, that is only the trigger. It is the automatic thoughts or, if you prefer, the connections you have made in the past that are now automatic and are creating those emotions. They are called automatic because they seem to pop up out of nowhere. Most of the time, you will not even be aware of them and even if you are, you tend to just accept them as the truth. And that happens so quickly that you do not even consciously realize you are doing it.

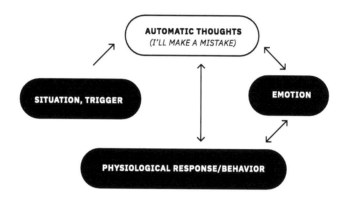

We owe this amazing discovery to Aaron Beck, one of the founders of the cognitive behavioral therapy. Each element of this model actually influences the others. For example, an automatic thought such as "What if I make a mistake..." creates a stress reaction inside of you. That emotion/stress produces a physical reaction that makes you have another thought: "I'll never be able to play with my hands shaking so much", and that makes you feel even more stressed etc. The arrows show the interconnected and interactive influence of each element, as if each component can feed the others.

The first step is about becoming conscious of this dance; to recognize it so that you can interrupt this automatic process and create a new pattern of response. Your ability to identify the early signs of stress will help you react differently.

"Between stimulus and response there is a space. In that space is our power to choose our response. In our response lies our growth and our freedom."

Viktor E. Frankl

Such automatic thoughts happen outside of our consciousness most of the time, and they are our first clues to uncover. They may sound like:

I always suck at auditioning.
I'm not ready.
What will people say?
I'm afraid to fail, to make mistakes.
I'll never make it as a professional.

Beck refers to these as our surface-layer of thought—thoughts being the general appellation for thoughts, beliefs and inner rules. These are conclusions that you automatically make because you have learned in the past that it is the way life works for you.

Beck proposes a hierarchy of three different levels of thoughts:

The automatic/surface thoughts, i.e. the phrases that come up most often and you ruminate on the most.

Intermediary beliefs take the form of obligations and rigid rules such as, I must be impeccable to deserve to go on stage, I should be able to do this easily by now, or, if I make a mistake people will make fun of me.

Core beliefs are the deepest structure of beliefs or schema that operates outside our consciousness, as in, I'm incompetent, I'm not enough, or everything is my fault.

Once we understand how we create our stress/emotion, automatically, we can deactivate that process and create a different outcome.

1. Downward arrow/Worst case scenario:

If you are interested in digging into your deeper structure and identifying your different beliefs, I would suggest David Burns's downward arrow method. You simply question the worst-case scenario: What is the worst that can happen? Or my favorite question, what are you afraid of? And then you ask after each answer, what will that mean for you? Or why would that be so bad?

For example, if the first thing that comes up is: I'll make a mistake.

- Ok, if that happens, what will that mean for you?

- That I'm a bad pianist.

- Ok, that seems a bit exaggerated but let's continue, if you're a bad pianist why would that be so bad?

- That would mean I don't deserve to be on stage.

- And if that were true, what would it mean for you? That would bother you because?

- It means I'm a failure and I'll never do anything in life. And I'll finish homeless, alone etc. You can play with these answers with many different questions to bring out the exaggeration, the dramatization and the lack of coherence. You may end up laughing and realizing that it makes no sense. For example:

- So if I understand well, if you make a mistake that means you're a failure?

- Making a mistake necessary means that you're a bad pianist?

- Does that mean that every pianist who make a mistake on stage doesn't deserve to be there? Or that they are bad pianists?

- Does failing necessarily mean that you'll never do anything in life? Or finish homeless?

In summary:

Situation/trigger = _____

Automatic thoughts = _____

If that happens, then it means that....

If ...., then.....

If.........that would bother me because.....

Why would that be a problem for you?

Is that the worst thing that you can imagine happening?

In the end, it is a good idea to explore your coping mechanism. If that were to happen, which we agree is very unlikely, what would you do? What are your options? In that example, if you make a mistake, how do you react? What do you do? Another example would be if you "fail" that audition/competition, what would you do after? How would you handle it? Take also time to ask yourself: how likely is it to happen? And finally, explore what is your best case scenario of this situation? We spent so much time worrying about what might go wrong that we forget to create a clear mental representation of our ideal performance.

In summary:

Worst case scenario?

What do you do if it happens?

How likely is it?

Best case scenario?

2. The Work

Usually, I question the first two or three automatic thoughts that come up with Byron Katie's method called "the work". This very simple yet extremely powerful process uses four questions and a turn around. It is a way to clear your mind. It is about taking responsibility for the war in your mind caused by your unquestioned thoughts.

Based on the same premise as Beck's model, i.e. that your thoughts create your emotional response, by questioning the validity and the veracity of those thoughts, you will be able to free yourself from them. Who would you be without your story? Because, as Byron Katie says: when I believe my thoughts, I suffer, when I question them, it stops. This process uses a meditative presence, a mindfulness attitude for each question. Be still and listen.

The recipe is very simple:

Is it true?
Can you absolutely know that it is true?
What happens and how do you react when you believe that thought?
Who would you be without that thought, if you never had that thought ever again?
Turn it around and find three genuine examples of how each turnaround is true in your life. That will bring out the evidence and the proof that your brain needs to open itself to this new perspective.

For example, if I use one of the fears I hear often, that I am afraid I will make a mistake.

Ok, **is that true?**
Then wait for the answer to come from a deeper part of yourself. Take time to ask that question with the intention of listening, of opening your heart like an invitation with kindness. It is the meditative part of this process that makes it so powerful.

Can you absolutely know that it is true?
Be very gentle and loving with yourself, be still, listen and wait. Be curious, be honest. There is no right or wrong answer. Maybe the answer is yes, maybe it is no.
Answer: Maybe I will, maybe I will not make a mistake. Ok, then is it true that you will make a mistake? No.

What happens when you believe that thought?

Most likely, you become stiff, anxious, you imagine all sorts of negative scenarios, you activate your survival response big time. Take a moment to feel what this thought or belief does inside your body and write down all the stuff it creates.

Who would you be without that thought?

Take time to imagine how you would feel?

Where in your body would it be different?

What would you tell yourself?

What would people notice that is different about you?

Turn it around:

"I will play wonderfully!" Ok, give me three examples in your life that prove it is true. Maybe you played those pieces beautifully by yourself or for someone else. I am sure you have two other specific moments when you played well in the past. Maybe you remember a performance that was very exciting or amazing and yet it was not, because you didn't make any mistakes. Those memories will show your mind that your initial thought is just subjective and not a reality.

Sometimes we can come up with two or three different turn-arounds.

It could be as simple as recognizing everybody makes mistakes. Give me three examples of that thought, maybe you saw a great musician you admire making some sort of mistake, and although you noticed them, it did not diminish the admiration you have for that musician. Maybe the singer that won the last competition made some mistakes and still won.

If the disturbing thought were something like "that judge does not like how I play", the turnaround could be, "I like how I play" and give me three examples proving that it is true—like three moments when you liked how you played.

If a musician mentions that his/her automatic negative thoughts are "if I make a mistake that means I'm a bad pianist and I don't deserve to be on stage, and if I make a mistake I'll feel like a failure or I'm afraid I'll never do anything in life," etc. then I would question all those answers with the four questions recipe:

I am a bad pianist (Is that true? Can you absolutely know that it is true?)

I do not deserve to be on stage. (Is that true? What happens when you believe that thought?)

I am a failure, I will never do anything in life. (Really? Turn it around?)

To help you with this disidentification process, I suggest that you go through these questions in writing because it will help stabilize your thinking. Your mind is very smart and will quickly play tricks on you. It will either get around or even dodge the question because it does not want to let go of the story it has been believing for so long.

I often use this evidence-based process to question what you are most afraid people will say about you or about your performance. The best preparation you can have is to face ahead of time the worst possible scenarios and deactivate the emotional charge by answering what will you do if it happens? And how likely do you think this may happen?

It is extremely powerful to realize that the cause of our own suffering is not the situation or a person, it is our thoughts about it. It takes courage to go inside ourselves and explore our darkness. Use those four questions as a flashlight. Remember: It is not because you have a though that it is necessarily true.

In summary:

Is it true?

Can you absolutely know that it is true?

What happens and how do you react when you believe that thought?

Who would you be without that thought, or if you never had that thought ever again?

Turn it around and find three genuine examples of how each turnaround is true in your life (evidence or proof).

3. Don't go NUTS with Stress

When I give a workshop, I start the segment on facing your fear with Dr Sonia Lupien's discovery to smoothly ease into that process and to break down the resistance that sometimes arises when we start investigating fears.

In her book, *For The Love Of Stress*, Dr Lupien mentions that after many years of research, she came to the conclusion that there are only four situations triggering a stress response in our life. She proposes a simple process to examine our triggers and help us transform that stress.

Those four triggers are grouped under the acronym NUTS. It stands for Novelty, Unpredictability, Threat to the ego and Sense of control.

N = novelty; when something new takes you out of your comfort zone.
U = unpredictability; when the situation occurs unexpectedly, like a surprise that catches you off guard.
T = threat to the ego; when you have the feeling that your competence is questioned or that your sense of self is threaten.
S = sense of control; when you are under the impression that you have little or no control in a situation.

First step: Deconstruction

Ask yourself: On a scale of zero to ten, your next audition is making you nervous because...
It is new? You do not do auditions often?
It is sudden or unexpected?
A part of you feels threaten and afraid?
You have no control over the situation?

For example, maybe under Control you rated 7/10, maybe you feel that you do not have control over what the jury is looking for, what they think, how the other competitors will perform or even how you will play.

Under Novelty you wrote 0, because you have done many auditions and you have many reference points for that type of situation.

Under Unpredictability, 3/10; you found out about that audition a week ago, so it is a little sudden but not a lot.

Under Threat of your ego 7/10, you have some fear of not being prepared enough, and you are afraid to make mistakes.

Second step: Reconstruction

Take the strongest trigger and ask yourself: What can I do to make this a little better, a little more comfortable? Not enough to take it from 7/10 to 0 but just a little less.

In this example, what could you do to go from Loss of Control 7/10 down to maybe a 6? Perhaps you can accept that certain things are out of your control. If it is not up to you, you can remind yourself why you make music and make a decision to focus on what your job really is, like your goals of action. Maybe you realize that you may not have control over certain aspects, but you have control over how you want to react, and you make a decision that no matter what happens, this audition is to test your new preparation tools. You will focus on feeling centered and in your bubble all the way through the performance. Each time something is not totally satisfying, you use your implantation of intention or use your key words.

You were also afraid of not being prepared enough and making a mistake at 7/10. What can you do, think, or say to yourself to help you go down to 6/10? If you still have a few days, maybe there are a few things that you really need to work on and that is the right time to apply some finishing touches.

Or maybe you need to have a clearer plan about mistakes. It could be accepting that we all make mistakes but how do you want to react when you make one? If it is a wrong note you keep your focus forward, there is nothing you can do about it. If it is a bigger mistake, you will test a new approach: stay calm, say to yourself "that's fine, I've got this", or "instead of tightening up, I look up and feel the air behind my nose" and get back on your feet.

Maybe you want to remind yourself that you are the worst judge of what is happening during a performance. Have you ever made a mistake in the past that felt like a catastrophe and when you hear the recording afterward you were surprised that it was barely noticeable? Your job is to play (or sing), not to judge how you are doing. You can focus on your actions and do the best you can with as much pleasure as possible.

Another way to use this tool is by comparing how you tend to react in different situations. You can get a general idea of your triggers by using the list of stressful situations proposed here or adapt it to your own needs, and rate each of these situations with a scale of zero to ten. I often do this general overview in workshops, and it is always fascinating to see that the same seemingly stressful situation produces totally different reactions in different people.

In summary:

FIRST STEP : ON A SCALE OF 0 TO 10.

STRESSFULL SITUATION	N	U	T	S
AUDITION				
RECITAL				
COMPETITION				
EXAMEN				
OTHERS				

Second step: What can I do to make the stronger triggers a little better? A little more comfortable?

With the first step, you can figure out what needs to be explored more in depth. For the second step, you can also use a different approach—like Emotional Intelligence.

4. Emotional Intelligence

Along with the importance of precisely labeling our emotions comes the promise that once we do give them a name, our feelings can provide useful information. They can be beacons, not barriers.

Susan David [20]

Emotional intelligence is a revolutionary concept developed by John Mayer and Peter Salovey at the beginning of the 1990s but made famous and accessible by Daniel Goleman's 1995 book, *Emotional Intelligence: Why it Can Matter More Than IQ.*

The general idea is to develop the skill to recognize and name emotions as they manifest themselves, to understand and draw a conclusion that will help you better cope with them.

In her book *Éloge de la joie de vivre*, psychologist Jocelyne Bélanger compares emotion to the dashboard light in a car that shows that something needs attention. We would never consider covering the light with one hand and ignoring it, hoping that it will turn off all by itself. It is the same with emotion. It is the signal that the unconscious brain uses to let us know that something needs our attention. The intelligence of the emotion appears when we take time to listen to the message behind our emotions, and find the real need hiding there.

Let us imagine that you have to go alone at night through a dangerous part of town, and you feel uncomfortable. This feeling is trying to pass on a message. It will urge you to find a solution like taking another route, jumping in a taxi, postponing to the next day or maybe even not going to that place at all. The message behind this emotion is to protect

20   Susan David, *Emotional Agility*, P.85

you, to make you react, and force you to use the best way possible to ensure your safety. Emotions are like ocean waves: they will not disappear, but you can learn to surf on them.

Here is my four-step recipe; it is based on the four necessary skills to develop your emotional quotient, as proposed by Salovey and Mayer:

- The ability to recognize emotions
- The ability to understand the natural progression of emotions
- The ability to think through (draw a conclusion from) your own emotions and those of others
- The ability to manage your emotions and those of others

Fear being one of the most debilitating emotions for performers, I will use it to demonstrate this process, but keep in mind that it works with all uncomfortable emotions.

Step One: Name the Emotion
(Recognizing Emotions)

Knowledge is power, as they say.

The first step demands some courage. If you are like me, once discomfort settles in, you may have a tendency to ignore it. In some situations, just by pretending that "it's not there" can make it go away. At other times, the old French saying «Ce à quoi je résiste, persiste» (what I resist, persists) takes on its full meaning. The emotion takes up more and more space until it forces us to stop and take the time to look into ourselves in order to understand what is really going on. We have to stay with this feeling just long enough to find the right words to express it. We welcome the emotion without judgment and give it the space it needs to deliver its message.

Sometimes to go faster, we have to slow down.
Popular saying

He who takes his time never lacks it.
Mikhail Bulgakov

What exactly frightens you? Each one of us will name his or her fear differently, and it is very important to find the words that are meaningful to you.

For example, are you afraid of:

- Making a mistake?
- Having a memory lapse?
- Being humiliated?
- Not being up to standards?
- Crashing?
- Being a fraud?
- Being on automatic pilot?
- Being judged?
- What people will think.
- Feeling paralyzed? Frozen?
- Judging and doubting yourself throughout your performance.
- Hitting a wrong note.

If you need inspiration, keep in mind that there are three big fears that always arise: fear of failure, fear of judgment (not being good enough), and fear of success.

Identifying your fear will give you just enough distance from it to establish communication and even to start translating the message it sends. With that distance, you will realize that you *have* this fear, not you *are* this fear.

If you are dealing with several fears, take the time to assess them all, and sort them according to how strong and disturbing they are. Once they are in order of importance, you may realise that they have a shared message or carry individual nuances. Begin dialoguing with each, starting with the strongest, it might disarm the others.

Step Two: The Somatic and Symbolic Manifestation
(Understanding the Natural Progression of Emotions)
Your unconscious mind communicates with you through sensations, images, and symbols. That is why I suggest that you gather the information also in a symbolic language. This will allow you to understand somatically, in a way that does not just use your logic, the natural progression of emotions.

Take note of how the fear manifests itself in your body, puts into words what you feel physically, and where exactly in the body it happens.

For example:

- Do you feel your stomach contract and tighten? Does it feel empty or full? Heavy or light?
- Are you agitated and ready to explode, or paralyzed and without emotion?
- Do you feel hot or cold?
- How is your posture? Your breathing?
- Does your chest feel tight? Or like a big rock?
- Do you feel like your head is empty, or too full?
- Are you thinking in slow motion, or so fast that you can't stay still?

And then, what is the symbolic representation of all these physical manifestations? What image or symbol best represents what you are going through?

For example:

- Do you feel like a headless chicken, or like you are underwater?
- Do you feel like a terrible beast is approaching?
- Or as if a big black cloud was stopping you from moving forward?
- Maybe your symbol is just a colour or a shape, like a glowing red circle?
- What is the best image to describe what is happening inside of you?

I know that answering these questions is not always an easy process. Fear, like most uncomfortable emotions, prefers to dwell in the darkness. But whenever you build a clear representation of what you fear, you dissociate from it. Once it has been identified, physically and symbolically represented, you can distance yourself from it. It then becomes much easier to understand what is happening, and you can discover the real intention behind this emotion.

Step Three: The Message
(Thinking Through Your Emotions/Draw a Conclusion)
The beast is just tamed enough for you to move on to the main step of the process:

uncover the message behind the emotion. Behind each fear hides a desire, a wish, a longing, a need. Many questions can help you figure it out. Depending on the situation or on that specific fear, you may find some helpful answer asking yourself what is the hidden desire? Or what is the need hiding behind that fear?

Ask yourself one or several questions from the following list and go deep down within yourself. Calm your inner dialogue and let an answer come up. This is not an intellectual exercise, but rather a way of opening up a channel of communication with your unconscious mind. Sometimes the answer comes right away; sometimes an intuition comes to you after a few hours; it may even take a whole night to manifest itself.

Here is the list of variations of the initial question "what is the message/what is the desire behind that fear?". Answer the ones that seem the most relevant to you:

- What is this fear telling you?
- If your fear could speak, what would it tell you?
- What is the message behind the surface?
- What does that imply?
- What is the need behind this fear?
- What is the good intention behind this fear?
- What is it trying to make you understand?
- What is the opportunity here for you? To do what? To be whom?
- What are you trying to prove? And to whom?
- What meaning do you give to what is happening to you right now?
- What are you afraid to lose?
- What are the advantages for you to feel stress or to be afraid?
- What will you gain to not reach your goal?

The message can be as simple as understanding that unconsciously, your expectations are exaggerated, and impossible to fulfil. Or that you have to forgive yourself for not being perfect, to accept your humanity. You have done all that you can, now you do your best, and that is all. Or perhaps it is a positive intention that speaks to you. This fear might be there to protect you, to make sure that you do not open up an old wound, and then you realise that it is ok, that wound is in the past. It is no longer necessary to avoid it. Maybe it is just an old habit and your desire to move forward is stronger. It becomes an opportunity, a chance to grow.

You know that you have found the right answer when your inner mood changes all of a sudden. A feeling of calm, relief, and clarity appears. You get the impression that you understood something important and gained control over your inner world.

Fourth Step: Decision or Action
(Managing Your Emotions)

To complete this process, now that you have gathered the relevant information, what decision will help you take care of yourself and make you feel better? What commitment will you make to yourself? When you understand what is going on inside of you, it is much easier to do something about it. It can be as simple as:

- Letting Go
- Accepting something
- Taking the decision to go forward or to postpone your performance
- Preparing differently
- Confirming an important element with another person, etc.

You can learn to outgrow your automatic response to stress and gain the perspective needed to reach beyond fight, flight or freeze. And even if some people consider fear to be a weakness, remember that it can also be a strength. It can help you clarify what you really want. As a wise man once said, "The bigger the goal, the greater the fear."

In summary:

1st Step: Name the Emotion
What are you afraid of, more specifically?

2nd Step: The Somatic and Symbolic Manifestation,
A. How does this emotion manifest itself in your body? And where?
B. What is the symbolic representation of these sensations?
    What image or symbol best represents what you feel?

3rd Step: The Message
What is the message behind this emotion?

What is its positive intention?

If this emotion could talk, what would it say, and what does it really need?

4th Step: Decision or Action

What decision or commitment do you take?

Here is an example of this process in action:

Just before the dress rehearsal of a concert, I was backstage with Adrian, a young professional baritone, when I noticed that he was not quite himself. I asked him what was going on, and he said that he felt bad because he was not as well prepared as he would have liked to be for this recital.

I offered to spend a few minutes with him to sort through the thoughts that bothered him, and he accepted with pleasure. I quickly explained the procedure for shedding some light on his discomfort, and I asked him the first questions of that four-step process.

"I feel guilty," he said, "like a little kid who's been caught doing something wrong. I feel that my upper body is contracted, tight, a little empty inside, and my head is almost in a panic."

He closed his eyes, and I asked him to stay in contact with this feeling just long enough to question him about its message. I asked him to welcome whatever comes up and explore all its possibilities.

What is the message behind the emotion, the hidden need? He told me that he really needed something... he would have needed more time. Little by little, he realized that he felt guilty that he took time to prepare another important project at the same time as this recital.

I asked him to look at these two projects from another perspective.

"What are you learning from what is happening now, that might help you next time?" I asked.

"I feel stuck because I would probably do the same thing, the two were important and I did the best I could, given the situation."

"That's cool. If it is too late to change the past, Adrian, what do you need right now?"

"I need to accept where I am at today. Maybe I made a mistake in calculating my preparation, but it's too late. It won't help me if I keep punishing myself with guilt."

"Great! What a wonderful realization! So what choices do you have now? Do you want to focus on what you are lacking, or on what you have?"

"I want to walk on stage with my strengths," he concluded, "and I want to connect deeply with the music. More than anything, I love sharing my passion for these pieces and all the emotions that I experience when I sing for people. Vocally I'm in great shape, and I really want to give this concert."

All of a sudden, his energy was transformed by a clearer motivation. He felt much better. We talked about the perfectionist in all of us, the notion of forgiveness, and I proposed the idea of accepting our imperfections in order to perform authentically. The result: he gave an amazing and inspiring recital, which had a lasting influence on him.

Concerning Guilt. When someone mentions guilt, I always have in mind a few basic rules to explore:

- What exactly did you do or say?
- Or what did you NOT do or did you NOT say?
- What is guilt moving you to do?
- What are you not accepting?
- Can you acknowledge that you made a mistake?
- What do you need to forgive yourself for?

If you accept what you have done or not done and you choose simply to learn from the event, you put aside judgment and are able to forgive yourself for being human. To grow is to learn from your mistakes and keep moving forward.

It sometimes happens that we don't feel prepared enough before a performance. In fact, we are rarely 100% ready. This often hides a fear of not being enough. When we accept that we could always have been more prepared, because preparation has no limit, we learn to trust ourselves and find peace and security in our ability to react rather than in the search to control all the possible parameters.

This extreme need for preparation is an unconscious rule from your inner perfectionist. You can never satisfy it with more preparation because that is not what it needs. The best way to break this vicious circle is to set realistic goals and make small, concrete steps towards them. That perfectionist side of you needs security, reassurance that you are doing well. Remind him that it is a journey and you are getting there one step at a time.

5. Self-compassion

~~~~~~

There will always be someone who can't see your worth. Don't let it be you.

Mel Robbins

~~~~~~

I chose to end this chapter on facing your fear with the ultimate weapon in your quest for optimal performance: self-compassion. The ramifications of self-compassion and what I talk about in this book, Flow, last minutes tools, your goals, calming your inner dialogue and facing your fears, are endless.

Self-compassion is generally defined as *a practice in which we learn to be a good friend to ourselves when we need it most-to become an inner ally rather than an inner enemy.*[21]

The first time I came into contact with this idea, it felt strange and I was doubtful. How can I be the best version of myself if I do not push myself hard and be very demanding? Being an overachiever, I always believed that if I am gentle and kind to myself I will be lazy and will not succeed. In fact, I found out that self-criticism may lead to short-term success but in the long run it slows me down.

Why criticism does not work

When we criticize ourselves, our alarm system initiates the fight or flight response and release the adrenaline and cortisol necessary to face the threat. Remember the reptilian part of our brain responsible for our survival? Well, with time it learned that imperfection or any fear of a potential imperfection is considered a real danger. With self-criticism, it is even more perverse because we are both the attacker and the attacked.

Fortunately, even if an ancient part of our brain is reptilian in origin, we are mammals. And the mammal's care system is unique because we are born immature. The infant needs to stay close to the mother to be safe. Our bodies are programmed to response to warmth and gentle touch. That releases oxytocin and opiates in our system, the feel-good hormones. Then it is normal to conclude that when we feel safe, reassured and loved, we are in the optimal mind state to do our best.

21 Germer, Neff, *The Mindful Self-Compassion Workbook, P.9*

After a disappointing performance, if your teacher or coach say I'm ashamed of you, you embarrassed me in front of everybody, you'll never do anything if you continue like this, you might go back and practice, but you are most likely to doubt yourself, feel rejected and sad, lose faith, become more afraid of failing again and spiral downward indefinitely.

Imagine that the teacher or coach says instead "I understand, it happens to all of us, I know you did your best. You're disappointed but I still believe in you, let me give you a hug. Don't worry, we'll get together tomorrow and figure out the next best step". That is the compassionate way.

Unfortunately, the first scenario is often only a shadow of what we tell ourselves after a performance. It is also a by-product of the self-esteem movement. Self-esteem can be a slippery road and misleading when build in comparison to others.

We associate self-esteem with feeling special and above average. You are special, you are unique, but everybody is. So, you cannot build it in comparison to others. It is drilled into our mind that to be average is an insult. But it is impossible that everybody is above average at the same time. And yet, I heard of a study on automobile drivers in California looking to measure their self-esteem in relation with their driving skill. Around 85% of the thousands of drivers who participated reported that their driving ability was above average!!!!!

Three essential elements of self-compassion:

An explosion of research into self-compassion in the last decade has shown so many benefits. Kristin Neff, one of the leading experts on this subject, defines self-compassion as having three core components:

Self-kindness: when we are as caring toward ourselves as we are towards others. To be encouraging, patient, gentle or simply treat ourselves with empathy, especially when we are having a rough day, because our tendency is to be harder and rigid with ourselves.

Common humanity: we are all interconnected in the sense that we all share the same human experience. To be human means that we all make mistakes. We are all a work-in-progress. When we struggle in life, we often feel as if something has gone wrong. We feel isolated and alone in our suffering when in fact that is our common link. The circumstances are different, the degree of pain is different, but the basic experience of human suffering is the same. Where self-esteem asks "how am I different from others?", self-compassion asks "how am I the same as others?"

Mindfulness: being aware of moment-to-moment experience, when we succeed in hacking our auto-pilot and are able to be with what is, in the present moment, to acknowledge and recognize that we are having a hard time and staying with that feeling long enough to respond with care and kindness. Instead of minimizing it (by denying or avoiding it) or exaggerating it, we get a more objective perspective of ourselves by being present.

The three reactions associated with the stress response, fight, flight or freeze, are the exact opposite of the three components of self-compassion:

We fight ourselves with self-criticism instead of being kind and caring with ourselves, by creating the feeling of reassurance and support we need.

We flee from others and isolate ourselves instead of opening up to feeling supported and connected in order to gain the social connection we crave.

We freeze when we engage in rumination (stay stuck in a loop about the negative aspects of a situation that is upsetting) instead of being present, mindful without exaggerating or denying what is happening in the now so that we can give ourselves the support we need to get better.

Each time we practice self-compassion, we are deactivating our alarm system and activating the care system. And when oxytocin and endorphins are released, they reduce stress and increase feelings of safety and security.

Just before a stressful performance, we want to be strong, to be courageous. Our tendency is to close ourselves and become hard as a shell. But to enter the Flow, we need to let go, to open up, to relax, to accept where we are as we are in that moment. The mindful-connected-kindness to ourselves will bring out a vulnerability that will open the door to the Flow.

Our imperfections are not inadequacies; they are reminders that we're all in this together. Imperfectly, but together.

Brené Brown

Self-compassion as another last-minute tool:

To bring self-compassion in every step of your performance preparation will have a great impact on your progress as well as your well-being in general. Here, I would like to propose a fun way to impact your brain's chemistry just before a performance. Just like some athletes have a playlist of songs or music that helps them contact the ideal inner state minutes before the event, you will prepare an updated, upgraded and improved version of a playlist, inspired by the three components of self-compassion, to watch and listen to before your next performance.

On your phone or your computer, you will prepare a slideshow that will include images or short videos that will evoke kindness, caring and connection with others. Here are a few examples, but make sure to adapt them to create your own personal triggers:

Someone holding a very young baby (care and kindness)
A father playing with or helping his son or his daughter (kindness and connection)
A beautiful starry sky, an amazing sunset or the Grand Canyon (connection with nature)
A beautiful garden with exotic flowers (care and connection)
A picture that makes you smile, either of love or of laughter (kindness)
A short funny clip like a blooper excerpt (kindness)
A social cause that is close to your heart (connection)
An athlete or performer who inspires you (connection)
A picture of Michael Jordan's poster with the motto: *If you run into a wall, don't turn around and give up. Figure out how to climb it!*
Or: *I've missed more than 9 000 shots in my career, I've lost almost 300 games, I've failed over and over in my life, and that's why I succeed.*

But first, you will start with a centering tool. You can use one of those Apps with a bubble that goes up, when you breathe in, and down when you breathe out, to calm and focus your mind. You will regularly bring back the App for ten seconds between the images you choose. End your slide show with an image or video that makes you smile or laugh. Then you are ready to perform.

In summary:
First: take a power pose like in the last-minute tools and hold that pose during the two or three minutes of your slide show.
Second: use the app to synchronize your breath and your mind for 30 seconds.
Third: start your slideshow, on a slow pace, maybe one picture every five to six seconds.
Fourth: you bring back the bubble App every 30 seconds for ten seconds, then back to more inspiring pictures.

Last: include funny pictures or videos to make you smile at the end.

If you want to add some music to your slide show, go ahead, make it inspiring for you.

6. Self-Compassion Post-Performance Tool: The Evaluation Grid

I have proposed many tools to prepare your performances, and now I want to introduce an evaluation grid to use after a performance. It will help you stay objective. And it is in synch with the mindfulness attitude and will help you develop a caring perspective as proposed by the self-kindness component.

The primary tool in this grid is the use of "Scale Questions". You will evaluate your performance and write down all the things you liked and didn't like. Those elements are your criteria: what is important for you when performing.

The criteria can be physical, technical, musical, or emotional. Each element will then be rated on a scale of 0 to 10, 10 being an ideal result. For example, you might find that you are rather satisfied with your performance. That is great, on a scale of 0 to 10, let us say 7. For each criteria, the scale will help you get in touch with a more objective evaluation. That is the mindfulness element.

The second step involves putting on "positive glasses" first. What was good about that 7? Why is it not a 5, for example? You might be satisfied with several things, like your level of calm, concentration, memory, spontaneity, connection with emotions, physical tension etc. Rate each one and why. That is the self-kindness touch.

The third step is precision. For example, if staying calm is important for you, how would you evaluate your level of calmness on a scale of 0 to 10? In which piece or at what moment exactly were you calmest? How do you explain it? What helped you to stay calm?

If you are anything like the musicians I work with, the first things you will come up with are all the things that did not go so well. But I insist and ask them to find three things that they liked first. To help them bring out the positive, I make an analogy with how a child learns to walk.

Do we tell them "No, no, not like that, you'll never get it! You're not straight enough! Keep your weight on your two feet!" It is rather the opposite, isn't it? At the smallest sign of a first step, everyone around them is thrilled, like they were watching a miracle. The toddler falls, and yet everyone keeps encouraging him, surrounds him with love. And yet, it will take months and even years for the child to perfectly master this new sense of balance.

Besides, when do parents give up and say, "He can't do it, he'll never walk"? After

13 months? 15 months? 20 months? They never give up, even if the child takes more time than others. And guess what? Aside for some genetic predisposition, all children learn to walk. What if you did the same thing with yourself now, with lots of encouragement and giving yourself time? (Remember self-compassion?)

When I work with someone who cannot find anything good in what he or she has just done, I trick his or her inner perfectionist by modifying the question. I can use for example: "What was better?" Or "What has improved since yesterday? Compared to your last performance, or compared with six months ago, what has gotten better?" And as a last resort, I also use the formula: "What was 'least bad' about it?"

Getting in touch with your "good moves" means recognizing your strengths. It is like telling your unconscious, "Next time, I am bringing all these good moves to my performance, and I will add a few more. I am building on what is good. I am adding, instead of focusing only on what is missing".

Once this update is done, I investigate what was "least satisfying", being as specific as possible, and using the scale for each element written down. Notice that I did not ask what was bad about it.

Nothing is bad. Talking about what is or was bad involves making a judgment. If there are things that you would like to do differently, how exactly would you like to do them? What do you have to do or put in place to get there? Keeping in mind this idea of "one step at a time." If you are at 4 out of 10, what could you do, to go up to 4.5 or 5 the next time?

In summary:

To be done in the 12 hours following the performance.
Write down observations only, no judgments.

1ˢᵗ Step

Give yourself the permission to express your emotional reaction following the performance. Once the dust has settled a bit, you can move on to the second step.

2ⁿᵈ Step

Make a list of your observations in two columns.
Be as specific as possible, move through each piece, even each part of each piece, with a fine-toothed comb, keeping in mind your criteria: technique, musicality, emotion, according to your initial goals.

What worked well?
What are you happy with, proud of? (Name at least three good things)
What did not work so well?
What was not satisfying?

Scale Questions
Each element is evaluated on a scale of 0 to 10 where 10 is the best possible result.

3rd Step
Change each unsatisfying point into a realistic, attainable goal for next time. What will you do differently? To go from 3 to 4, for example, to get just a little better.

Conclusion
What do you learn from this experience, both from what worked well and from what was less satisfying?

I CAN'T DO THIS ANYMORE

As the head coach of l'Atelier Lyrique de l'Opéra de Montréal, I often work with aspiring young pianists who want to become vocal coaches. One Sunday afternoon, after a concert where Florence, a young pianist, had accompanied 12 singers in almost thirty excerpts (yes, a real marathon), she said to me, "I played so badly, I am so discouraged, I can't do it anymore."

I was happy to have been at the concert because my perception of her performance was very different than hers. I told her that I had liked the concert a lot, that I did not want to downplay what she was going through, and that I would like to talk with her in an hour or two when the dust had settled.

She called me after supper. She was calmer, but still just as disappointed about the concert. I suggested that we examine what happened in a little more detail.

"Overall, for the whole concert, what would you give yourself on a scale of 0 to 10, 10 being extraordinary?"
"Um, 3!"
"Okay! Let's have a closer look if you don't mind" I said. "How was the first piece?"
"It was all right, not bad."

"On a scale of 0 to 10?"

"Probably an 8."

"Excellent. How was the second piece?"

"A nightmare!"

"On a scale of zero to ten?"

"3!"

"Okay. How was the beginning?"

"I messed up the introduction, I played a wrong note, and I didn't know what tempo to take."

"What does that experience allow you to learn?"

"What did I learn? Urgh, I'm not sure I understand."

"What could you do tomorrow or in the coming days so that next time will be more satisfying?"

"Well, I need to look at the fingering in the introduction, specially, the third measure of the intro, and since it's a new piece, I haven't done it enough with the singer, I need to run through it with her a few times to make sure we're both comfortable with the tempo."

"Excellent. And the rest of the piece was all right?"

"Yeah, it was just a question of tempo. If I play it a few times, it'll fix itself. Now I realize, maybe it was 6 out of 10 instead of 3."

"Super. How was the third piece for you?"

"I'm not sure, I think it went well, but I was doubting myself while I played."

"I think I have a clue for you," I said. "In the concert hall, I found the balance between the voice and the piano was a little strange. The piano could have been a little more present. I had the impression that you were afraid to overpower the singer, but in my opinion, it was the opposite, you weren't too loud, it was just a bit too soft, so you could have played more.

"That's it! I was holding back, I hesitated...."

"What can you do, what would be helpful in order to prepare for next time?"

"I only have to play the piece once tomorrow, a little slower, without holding back, and think about not holding back just before playing it next time."

"And if you aren't holding back, what are you doing?" (Just to formulate it positively),

"I play into the bottom of the keys, I release each chords, I sit back strait, and breathe more deeply."

"Very good! And the fourth piece?"

"The fourth was all right, I've played it many times before, I was comfortable. I'd say 9."

We went through the whole programme this way. After examining it for half an hour, Florence felt much better. She noticed that there were only five or six pieces out of 30 that were not satisfying, but since they were spread out throughout the concert, she had the impression that the whole concert hadn't gone well. This is why specificity is important.

I saw her the next day. She looked happy to have put things in perspective and went into her practice room with a clear and inspiring plan in mind. She knew exactly what she had to work on, and what to do to improve it. In a word, she was radiant.

CONCLUSION:
LET YOUR LIGHT SHINE THROUGH

Vulnerability is not winning or losing; it's having the courage to show up and be seen when we have no control over the outcome. Vulnerability is not weakness; it's our greatest measure of courage.

Brené Brown [22]

We have covered a lot of territory throughout this book. An inner journey towards the performance of your dreams. I wanted to share with you the results of my years of research and all my discoveries, hoping they will impact your life as much as they have mine.

It started with an expedition into Flow, and just as Mihaly Csiksentmihalyi stumbled on Flow while searching for the meaning of life and the secret of happiness, I believe that in the end, we are all looking for the same thing: happiness. But in this performance-oriented world, our desire to be our best can lead us to confuse success with happiness.

Success versus happiness

I was raised to believe that if I work hard, I will have success and I will be happy. Research in positive psychology and neuroscience has proven that it actually works the other way around—happiness is a precursor of success.

Success is what they call a moving target. As soon as you reach your goal, you may be happy for a few moments, but you tend to want very quickly something else. Success is a never-ending target that transforms itself as soon as you reach it. Happiness is in the journey and not a reward waiting at the destination.

Let me use Shawn Achor's metaphor to illustrate this: Many years ago, everybody believed that the earth was at the center of our universe and that the sun and all the planets gravitated around us. It took Copernicus to demonstrate with complex mathematical calculations that the sun was actually at the center of our universe, and that position explained the movement of all the planets.

22 Brené Brown, *Rising Strong,* P.4

We have the same misconception with success and happiness. We tend to put success at the center of our universe thinking that happiness is a by-product, a result of reaching success when actually, it has been proven that it is the other way around. It is when happiness is at the center, when happiness is our sun, then everything else including success, emanates from it.

Happiness becomes the fuel and the goal. Instead of delaying happiness while concentrating on achieving a goal, happiness would be the rocket fuel, and a big advantage to tap into our maximum potential.

Too often, people confuse happiness with pleasure. They think if something is not fun, pleasurable, then they are not happy. It is not exactly true. Pleasure is about a punctual satisfaction of a short duration whereas happiness is an inner state more stable and durable. That is why you can be working on a long-term project, having very challenging and even difficult moments, and still feel happy.

That explains why happiness is defined sometimes as the *"joy we feel striving after our potential."*[23] And I like to add that happiness is when you have no desire to be somewhere else or do anything else. That means it is not so much what you do but the reason why you are doing it. Happiness is about finding meaning in what you do. A meaningful life comes from growing, a sense of progress just as when you are walking a path towards your potential.

And because the number one predictor of success is a strong social connection, when your meaningful life includes a sense of contribution, your wellbeing is even more guaranteed—it is no longer just about you, it is about us, about what makes you feel connected to others. Your potential, your gift is shared for a cause greater than yourself.

Since this book is dedicated to help you unleash your full potential, I will leave you with my take on charisma.

The word charisma comes from the Ancient Greek "Kharisma", meaning "gift", in the sense of a favor, a divine blessing. A gift is not something you learn, not something you deserve, it is given to you. It is for you, a divine gift means it is your true nature. That implies it is in you already.

Those we encounter who have charisma, that special quality of presence, let themselves be seen. They let their divine gift shine through. They are not forcing, imposing a certain attitude, being rigid and controlling about what others will perceive of them. It is

23 Shaun Achor, *The Happiness Advantage*, P.40

more like an openness, a vulnerability and an authenticity. We associate it with self-confidence, as in an inner coherence that comes from being at peace with who we are. When we are in contact with our true nature, our uniqueness shines, without hiding it or flaunting it.

There is and there will only be one of you, just like your finger print. That presence to share your precious inner light, to let your life force shine in all its glory. Nothing upstages us more than a smiling baby because its light shines through. Its life force is unobstructed because it does not yet know how to do otherwise. Whether it is happy or angry, the switch is on.

We are all meant to shine, not just some of us, but everyone. And the most beautiful part is that when we finally do, our own light gives the permission to others to do the same, otherwise the gift is lost.

Our deepest fear,

Our deepest fear is not that we are inadequate. ∪
Our deepest fear is that we are powerful beyond measure. ∪
It is our light, not our darkness
That most frightens us. ∪

We ask ourselves
Who am I to be brilliant, gorgeous, talented, fabulous?
Actually, who are you not to be? ∪
You are a child of God. ∪

Your playing small ∪
Does not serve the world. ∪
There's nothing enlightened about shrinking ∪
So that other people won't feel insecure around you.

We are all meant to shine, ∪
As children do. ∪
We were born to make manifest ∪
The glory of God that is within us. ∪

It's not just in some of us; ᴜ
It's in everyone.

And as we let our own light shine, ᴜ
We unconsciously give other people permission to do the same. ᴜ
As we're liberated from our own fear, ᴜ
Our presence automatically liberates others.

Marianne Williamson, A Return To Love

References

Shawn Achor, *The Happiness Advantage*, 2010, Crown Business

Shawn Achor, *Big Potential*, 2018, Crown Publishing Group,

J.S. Beck, *Cognitive Behavior therapy*, 2011, The Guilford Press

Brené Brown, *Rising Strong*, 2017, Penguin Random House

Brendon Burchard, *High Performance Habits*, 2017, Hay House, inc.

Steven Chandler, *100 Ways to Motivate Yourself*, 2012, Career Press

Mihaly Csikszentmihalyi, *Flow the psychology of optimal experience*, 1990, Harper Perennial/Harper Collins Publishers,

Susan David, *Emotional Agility*, 2016, Penguin Random House

Jonathan Fader, *Life as Sport*, 2016, Da Capo Press

C. Germer, R. Siegel, P. Fulton, *Mindfulness and Psychotherapy*, 2013, The Guilford Press

C. Germer, K. Neff, *The Mindful Self-Compassion Workbook*, 2018, The Guilford Press

Don Greene, *Performance Success*, 2002, Routledge

B. Katie, *Who Would You Be Without Your Story?* 2008, Hay House Inc.

S. Kotler, *The Rise of Superman*, 2014, Amazon Publishing

R.L. Leahry, *Cognitive Therapy Techniques*, 2017, The Guilford press

Olivier Lockert, *Confiance et Estime de soi avec l'hypnose*, 2012, Edition IFHE

Sonia Lupien, *Well Stressed (For the Love of Stress)*, 2014, Harper Collins

Paul McKenna, *I Can Make You Confident*, 2010, Sterling Publishing Co. Inc

S.M. Orsillo, L.Roemer, *Worry Less, Live More*, 2016, The Guilford Press

M. Robbins, *the 5 Second Rule*, 2017, Savio Republic Book

M. A. Singer, *the Untethered Soul*, 2007, New Harbinger Publications, Inc.

When Passion Leads to Excellence: the case of musicians
Bonneville-Roussy, Lavigne and Vallerand, Psychology of Music 2011 39:123
DOI: 10.1177/0305735735609352441

Deakin, J.M., Cote, J., & Harvey, S. A. The Influence of Experience and Deliberate Practice on the Development of Superior Expert Performance. The Cambridge handbook of expertise and expert performance. 2006. (38) 683- 700.

Acknowledgement

I want to sincerely thanks Howard Aster of Mosaic Press, for his offer to write a book specifically for singers and instrumentalists. All I was looking for, was to publish in English my first book, written for general public. Thanks to him, I ended up putting together a much more appropriate and up-to-date manual that I think will have a greater impact on musicians. On this subject, I really want to thank «Les Éditions de l'Homme» for allowing me to use some material published in *Atteindre sa zone d'excellence*.

I feel privileged to have had the help and support of several wonderful friends, for so many years. Thanks to Pierre, Pascal, Jocelyne, Marc... and I want to thank more specially Éthel Guéret and Lise Beauchamp, my first proof-readers, for their unfailing support through this whole adventure of performance preparation and for their inspiring feedback of the manuscript.

My sincere gratitude to Matthew Nini for his patience in the first step of translating in English *Atteindre sa zone d'excellence* even if I ended up using only 20% of that material. A very warm thanks to Judith Bédard who, one year later, helped me refine and optimize the last version of the manuscript. I also want to thank Benoit Massé for his wonderful drawings. They bring a lightness in this very dense and sometimes intense material.

And finally, a special thanks to all the singers and instrumentalists who attended my workshops and conferences. Their curiosity and questions have helped me clarify and discover so many new ways. Thanks to them, I continue to grow, to refine and expand this never-ending quest of performance preparation.

About the Author

French Canadian vocal coach Claude Webster, has been internationally sought after as a leading specialist in French repertoire. Since 2004, he has been invited every year to the International Vocal Arts Institute in Tel-Aviv. He has also been on faculty at programs in Berlin, New York, Miami, Ravinia, Puerto Rico, Montreal, Toronto and Virginia. He was the head coach at Opera de Montréal's young artist program «L'Atelier lyrique de l'OdeM» from 1997 to 2017.

Claude Webster's diverse skills have led him to be involved at l'Opéra de Montréal in numerous capacities. He has been the pianist/répétiteur for over 50 productions and is the Chorus master since 2007.

Constantly looking for new ways to help singers, he specialized himself in performance preparation. He holds a certificate in psychology from the Université du Québec à Montréal (UQAM) and is also a certified professional Neuro Linguistic Programming (NLP) coach and instructor as well as a Professional Certified Coach (PCC) with the International Coaching Federation (ICF).

He regularly gives lectures and workshops in colleges and conservatories on stress management and mental preparation for performances. He published a book «*Atteindre sa zone d'excellence*» (Reaching you inner zone of excellence) based on his workshops; and is now proposing a handbook written specifically for singers and instrumentalist.

NOTES

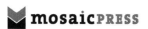